Dear Mother

Dear Mother

Letters to my Mother in Spirit

Mystic Ed

The Happy Medium and Psychic to the Stars

BLUE DRAGON PRESS

Dedicated to

Phyllis Margaret,

My Mother

First published in 1997 by
Blue Dragon Press Limited,
Unit 9, The Old Water Yard,
Curtis Road, Dorking, Surrey RH4 1EJ

Design and typesetting by Aztec Design, Guildford, Surrey (UK)
Printed and bound by GoPrint, Guildford, Surrey (UK)

British Library Catalogue-in-Publication Data
A Catalogue record for this book is available from the British Library

ISBN 1 900 36524 3

Love is what we are

and
Without love we are nothing.
Out of the darkness will come light
Without the love of God we cease to exist.

May God bless all of you that read this book. May it help to guide you — and you to guide others who come into your lives.

Love and Light,

Yours,

Mystic Ed

Chapter One

New Year's Day, 1995

Dear Mother,

You'll never guess what's happened since you've been gone. I've become a household name — Mystic Ed, The Happy Medium, the Psychic to the Stars! I've got my own programme, my own show! But as I sit in bed writing to you I look at your photograph. You know — the small black and white one that's kept on Dad's side of the bed. Again, as I hold it in my left hand it slowly changes into colour. First your hair, auburn, and then your emerald green sweater. Now your eyes — heather mixture .... but as I gaze .... back it changes to black and white again. One of your ways of telling me and proving to me that you're still around and there for me. But as I gaze at your photograph, it makes me think back .... back .... back to that night, that terrible, terrible night when you passed over .... *and I wasn't there ....*

It's two years ago. Your cancer had returned, this time for the final time. I gave up work to care for you, to be with you. Right to the end. The illness that wrecked your whole body wrecked my whole life. You went from nine and a half stone down to five stone in a matter of a few months — and yet you still had hope. Still, your face was beautiful and your love for me shone through the darkness of that terrible time. I recall how I used to lie on my bed listening to "Madame Butterfly" by Puccini — wanting to cry, to get it out of my system. But no. I couldn't.

'If anything ever happens to me you'll have to get yourself a cat,' you said. Even in times of distress a sense of humour continued.

(Well, I've got one now, Mother, and the scratches to prove it!)

Every day, every night was spent caring for you. Yet you know you were no trouble and every minute was a golden hour to have each other. But I knew it wouldn't be long before we were parted. Psychically speaking, I knew that within weeks you would be in Spirit. The doctors told me, you know. Coldly, I was told, 'Give it three months.' And I held this dreadful secret within my troubled, anxious mind. No one knew the awful truth. Then November came. It had been the most beautiful autumn I ever remembered. When you were well you always said, 'When I die I want to die in the autumn, when the leaves are falling.'

You were to have your wish.

So that I could recharge my batteries to prepare myself for what would be a horrifying end to your life you went to St. Giles' hospice. I took you there. Yet little did I realise that I was taking you to die. Your final journey. I remember the last time I saw you alive. I kissed your cheek and looked back and waved goodbye to you as I neared the doorway. But you didn't wave. You didn't smile. You just looked .... I just don't know what you were thinking and even now I cannot describe the look you gave me. It wasn't sad, wasn't happy, wasn't anything. You just looked .... and I walked away.

A feeling came over me, like a large black thundercloud and I didn't like it. I went shopping, getting a few things in for when you were to return home. I got back to the bungalow, changed your sheets and blankets so you would have a nice cosy bed to come home to. It was to be the last thing that I would ever do for you while you were still alive.

I couldn't sleep that night. The thought of you away from me scared me. Every night I always called to you: 'If you need me, just whisper and I'll be there.' So I called again, but this time there was no reply. Just an eerie silence. It's 1:30 a.m. and I finally doze off after taking a sleeping tablet.

I awake with a start. It's 2:40 a.m. The phone is ringing. I throw myself out of bed and answer it.

'It's St. Giles. You're mother's fighting for breath. She's calling for you. It's only a short time. Drive like mad — but .... be careful!'

I nearly drop the phone. I throw on some old clothes, race through the front door and into the car. Having to drive 30 miles through Cannock Chase to the other side of Lichfield can be dangerous to say the least. The roads wind up and down through the trees and I was driving at 100 mph. I don't know how I got there. *Keep awake, keep awake!*

'Oh God, no! *No!*'

'I don't believe this!'

I called out over and over: 'I've got to get there. I've just got to! Hang on!' Driving after a sleeping tablet is not to be recommended. I wound the window down, opened the sun roof, put the radio on, lit a cigarette .... I've got to keep awake .... got to .... oh, God .... *hang on!*

It's five to three in the morning. I've driven 30 miles in ten minutes. I drive to the back doorway of the hospice. Silence. Darkness. A door opens. Two nurses look at me. The looks on their faces tell me it's too late.

'No! .... It can't be ....'

'We're sorry. Come through. We'll make you a pot of tea.'

(Tea! I don't want BLOODY TEA!)

We sit drinking tea.

'Her heart gave out,' they tell me.

All I can think is, 'Too late. Five minutes too late.'

'When can I see my mother?'

'Anytime you wish.'

The shock hasn't hit me yet. We walk into the ward. They pull back the curtain. There you were. They had placed a beautiful salmon pink rose by your head. I could tell you'd gone and yet .... your Spirit was *there.* It hadn't quite left you. I sat down and held your hand.

'Leave me alone with her, please.'

The nurse left us together. THEN the shock hit me. I prayed to God. 'If I have the gift of healing, *please* let it come to me now.'

It was as though your hand was becoming warm again. Yet it was only the warmth of my hand holding yours. I cried, 'Forgive me!'

How selfish we all become at times of grief. It's true. Our whole lives flash before us and we think of the things we shouldn't have said, the things we shouldn't have done. And the things that we should have said, like, 'I love you with all my heart.'

But, Mother darling, it was, 'Forgive me for not being there for you .... just when you needed me most.'

Yet I know that if you could have answered me you would have said, 'But I didn't want to get you out of bed.'

I kissed your forehead. Held your hand.

Then an arm led me away.

'I've made you some more tea,' said the nurse.

She led me to the lounge. A huge room filled with settees and armchairs. Like something from a plush hotel.

I don't know why I was led there. I looked up at the clock. 4:15 a.m. I lit a cigarette and drank tea. Being in a huge room at 4:15 in the morning and knowing that your mother lies "asleep" in the next room is probably the loneliest and most traumatic experience anyone can imagine.

I smoke, I cry. I smoke, I cry more and more. Louder and louder. Over and over. I feel so alone. I can go back and see you for one final time. I have to wash my face and fingers first. I feel that you will "smell" cigarettes and I know how much you hated smoking.

I'm led back to you. Spiritually I have to look up. You are lying down .... and yet .... it's as though .... your Spirit is "above", looking down. I think back to a relationship I once had that wasn't meant to be.

'Where *are* you *now*? I need you so *much*!'

They're telling me that I have to go. They have to "move you" before the other patients wake up.

'Five minutes more, please.'

'Very well.'

Every day spent looking after you for months and months. We're parted for one day .... and you're taken from me. I know that you wouldn't have wanted me to have witnessed your passing over into Spirit. I wanted it for me. Don't a lot of us? While we were together you were holding on. For me. We were separated and my father called you to him. I place the pink rose in your hands.

'You have to leave now.'

I kiss your forehead. I get up to leave. I look back. So peaceful. So beautiful. I love you. I don't want to leave you. You were my life.

5 a.m. The world is silent. I drive slowly now until I reach the house of my dear friend Jess. I knock on the door. How can I be so bold as to wake her at this time? She doesn't come to the door. I sit on the wall by the car. I sit and wait. I knock on the door again. Jess, wondering what the hell's going on, peers through the curtains, sees me and opens the door.

'It's all over.'

I cry in her arms. Like a child.

Oh, the pain.

We spent the day together, arranging the funeral. Jess was wonderful. She felt for me as though she had lost her own mother. She couldn't have given me more support and I shall always love her.

That night I stood under the shower for three hours, wanting to wash away the negative aura that surrounded me.

It was then that you gave me my first sign of your existence. Being a talented classical pianist many years ago, that was one of the first things that shook me.

I sat in the front room in your armchair .... and then .... music .... *piano* music .... coming from somewhere, nowhere, anywhere. Beautiful melodies surrounding me. And then it stopped. I was comforted by that, Mother dear. Music from heaven. My first sign from you to make me realise that you still *lived on* and were doing what you loved most: playing the piano.

I shall never forget that next day. Even though your music was a sign, I grieved. I wanted to be with you. I know — and it's true — that should any of us take our own lives, that we take the suffering and the "not being able to cope" over into the next world. Not only may our Spirit become earthbound, but in our next life on earth we will have to endure the same traumas until we have learned to realise the *truth.* The truth being that we have to experience pain so we can appreciate true joy. Life is a classroom. If we don't learn the first time, we have to go back to the class until we've learned and earned a degree through many, many experiences.

Nevertheless, it's natural to have these feelings after someone has passed over. We wouldn't be human otherwise and there definitely is a time for us all to grieve at one time or another. We are allowed to do so! We have to learn to adjust to life without that person. Some people find it easy, some difficult. You, Mother, were my best friend, sister and mother all wrapped up into one.

I put on your green dressing gown and lay on your bed. And cried.

'Oh, Mother. Call me to you wherever you are. I'll be happy to join you. Call me. I'm only a whisper away.'

You didn't call. Instead, I heard your voice, 'Look in the dressing table. Left side. Top drawer.'

Another sign of your existence.

I dried my eyes and opened the drawer. I found your book of poems by Rudyard Kipling and a book of poems that you wrote as a child. And then I found *it*. The poem that answered my pleas of, 'Whisper and I'll come to you'.

WHISPER AND I SHALL HEAR

If in the Summer morn, dear, you wander amid the flowers
If you feel sad and lone, dear, thinking of past glad hours
Just breathe my name to the woodlands, sigh what your heart would say
I know I shall hear your message, dear,
Borne on the breeze away.

Oh, winds that blow from the South
Sighing so soft and low;
Whisper your secret sweet,
Whisper and I shall know.

If when you're weary, Darling, you wander at gloaming tide
Where by the stream and meadow we wandered side by side
Whisper you love me, Darling, say that your heart is true
Whisper you love me, Darling, just as you used to do.

Oh, winds that blow from the South
Sighing so soft and low;
Whisper your secret sweet,
Whisper and I shall know.
Oh, winds that blow from the South
Breathe in my listening ear;
Come from the heart of my love,
Whisper and I shall hear.
Come from the heart of my love,
Whisper and I shall hear.

I thank you with all my heart for that, Mother.

Isn't it sad when people don't bother to come and see you until it's too late? You were so unhappy about one particular relative who never came near you. You used to say, 'It'll be no good her coming to the funeral when I've gone, people need to see you when you're alive!'

Oh, how I felt for you. That relative couldn't be bothered to come even when invited. I used to say, 'One day, should anything happen to you, I shall tell her it's too late.' And that's what happened. I phoned her on the day you passed into Spirit, remember? I told her she was too late now. She then blamed you for 'not allowing me to tell her'. No sorrow. Hard as nails.

Months later I found out that this particular relative couldn't understand how she managed to get to your funeral. Apparently the car broke down ....!

After all, you did say that 'If she can't see me while I'm alive, she needn't come when I'm dead.'

(Not once has that lady been to see me since my mother's passing. I have been to see her myself — and regretted it. I tried to tell her about what type of work I am doing for Spirit and the answer was, 'I don't know how you think you're going to do THAT!' Time to walk away, I think.)

After reading your poem I was filled with an inner strength. The night before the funeral I visited you in the Chapel of Rest. I placed your crystal rosary between your fingers, combed your hair and anointed your forehead with frankincense oil. I knew then that your Spirit had gone. I sang *True Love* from "High Society" to you between tears, the song that you sang me to sleep with when I was a baby. Then I kissed you goodbye. You had a good funeral.

A week before your passing I had played Albinoni's "Adagio" on the organ while you lay poorly in bed. Afterwards you said, 'That was played so beautifully, it will haunt me till the day I die.' So it was played at your funeral. The church was decorated beautifully and only one thing was wrong. They called out your name as Phyllis *Mary* Ward instead of *Margaret.* (Later that year at a memorial service for all that had passed away that year they did the same again. The vicar said, 'Oh, well!')

Steve, a good friend of mine, was on one side of me, Jess on the other. You gave me strength to "get through".

So it was over, Mother. Where do I go from here? Another chapter is about to begin. Another door is about to open.

You're always around, but not physically. I called to you one night before I went to sleep and you appeared to me in my dreams. Remember?

'If I could come back to you, my darling, I would have to experience the very same end to my life again,' you said.

I woke up thinking, 'Well, I wouldn't want that for you, Mother. Better to be in Spirit and out of pain than on this earth plane and having to repeat the process.'

You're here for me, but I miss seeing you. AND I WISH I COULD HOLD YOU IN MY ARMS AGAIN.

Chapter Two

New Year's Day, 1995

Dear Mother,

When life hands you a lemon you have to make lemonade out of it. What will this year bring without you? Somehow I've got to fight on. I've just got to! Got through my first Christmas without you and yet your presence was very close all the way through.

I've tried to be strong so far, just as you would wish and it's difficult at times. Just before Christmas I was very low. Steve, my friend, was with me. It was his hand that reached out to mine as though to say "hold on". I've always looked upon him as my little brother. There's a bond between us that I can't explain. He had cancer too, non-Hodgkins lymphoma. Something keeps telling me I have work to do — spiritually. Can't think why. I know you're trying to tell me something, Mother. He's had all the hospital therapies now, including a bone-marrow transplant. Cancer could return today, tomorrow, twenty years on or never. Still, he's fine right now.

(I do stress most strongly that *any* form of illness should never be used by its name, since when we do the power of the word gives the illness control over us.)

I always knew that I had been blessed by God with the gift of Spiritual-healing. I can remember going up to people at bus stops and saying things like, 'You've got a cracking headache.' They would look at me, startled as to how I knew and the next thing I would be laying my hands on them — drawing away the pain and replacing it with peace and love. Something's telling me that I'm going to be doing a lot of healing before I'm finished. Nevertheless — like in your case, Mother — when it's your time, it's your time.

I've been thinking a lot about that type of thing since you passed over into Spirit. Do you remember a Sunday about twelve years ago .... *when you did?*

You looked magnificent that day as we arrived at the Christian Science Church in Wolverhampton. Dressed in your fur coat and sage green velvet dress, wearing your favourite amber jewellery. But you said you didn't feel "right". As though you were "slipping in and out of somewhere". As we sat through the lesson I could sense that things were not right with you. You weren't sitting "right". Then it happened. You said that you felt you were "going under". While the service continued, I managed to help you to stagger out into the foyer. A healer from the church named Mary (now also in

Spirit) came with us. Then you collapsed. It was sheer tragedy as I watched you "go" and then .... you breathed your last.

'Oh, no .... No!' I screamed as you slipped away. 'Come back .... *come back!*'

Mary looked at me. I looked at her. Our thoughts met.

'She's gone.'

'No! No! Come BACK!'

And then .... a miracle occurred. Your eyes opened. The greyness of your face went. Life returned to you, (one reading this cannot fully comprehend the moment). Later that day, as you rested in bed, you told me how you knew you'd "gone" but heard my voice pleading with you to come back. I suppose in a way I was there with you "at the end" — only it had happened many years before ....

Something's telling me to move on, Mother. I have a feeling within me. A strange excitement literally surging through my veins. I've started to be positive again knowing that I, like everyone else, have been given this precious gift of life and now it's time to turn every negative thing in life into the positive. To turn things around to your advantage. *When life hands you a lemon ....?!* It's time to realize that even when the worst has happened a new days always arrives with the chance for happiness to be. And the chance to go out and make someone smile. To touch someone's life with love.

I've got to think seriously now about what I'm going to do with the rest of my life. Find a career with purpose and also help other people. As you know, I was always psychic. Everything I said would always come true. Oh, and my dreams .... every one of them! And the auras I've seen around people, plants, everything .... There's certainly a good reason for all these things happening. There are no such things as coincidences. Every coincidence has a real meaning, good or bad. Yet with each coincidence comes learning, which transforms into experience. Experience becomes growth and therefore knowledge. Finally wisdom from which we can help, advise and teach others. Yes, that's what I must do. Help others!

'You're certainly unique, Ted,' you always said, especially after I had been crystal gazing for three hours at a time. I recall seeing only three months previously the face of my Canadian uncle, Uncle Ted, in the crystal ball. I couldn't understand why he was looking back at me. The next day I was in town when I ran into my godmother, Doreen.

'I think you ought to know,' she said. 'Your Uncle Ted passed on yesterday.'

After my vision, I wasn't exactly shocked by this. I remember thinking while she told me, 'He looked perfectly o.k. to me!'

Do you remember when I saw a man in Spirit at Grandmother's? I was nineteen then.

(My Grandmother Emma is now one of my guardian angels. Many mediums see this lady standing beside me.)

I was staying at Granma's while your sister Mavis was away on holiday. It was about 3 a.m. and I looked up from my bed to see a gentleman appear from "out of the wall" and walk right up to the bed. I can almost see him now.

Naturally I was startled (to say the least!) and buried my head under the bedclothes, heart beating like mad.

'Go away!' I yelled.

(It never ceases to amaze me why my best time for seeing Spirit is 3 a.m.! It's their choice what time they make an appearance, of course, and we have to remember that in Spirit our loved ones don't wear wristwatches!)

I woke up the next day with the name "Bob" going through my ears. I thought 'I can't tell Granma this, it will scare the life right out of her!' (And she was in her eighties, too!)

Yet that evening ....

Granma and I were sitting in front of the fire when suddenly she came out with a story that made my mouth drop open.

'I remember it vividly,' she began. 'Bob was the only man I truly loved. Yes, I did love your Grandfather Frank, but not in the same way I loved Bob. I was in love with him as soon as we met. But he doublecrossed me, two-timed me. He broke my heart. And it was because I was so vulnerable at the time that I married your grandfather. It was selfish of me really, but I thought that I was going to be left on the shelf. Years later Bob came to see me. He wanted me back. But it was too late. I was a married woman with a baby, your mother Phyllis, my eldest daughter. I had to let him go. And yet I loved him. And wanted him. But I was married ....' Granma paused and sighed sadly. 'So really my married years with your grandfather were bitter ones. I was pretty tough on him.'

She sighs again. I sit in silence and gaze into the fire while she continues. I feel the presence of Spirit all around me. I'm starting to get the picture.

'One night, during the war, I look up and see Bob .... coming up to my bed. "What are you doing here?" I called out, but he didn't reply. It was then that I realized I had seen his *Spirit.* I was petrified and threw the bedclothes over me. "Go away!" I yelled. I felt as though I was being strangled. A few days later I learned that on that night, in the war, he was strangled .... by his own parachute ....'

By this time my heart was pounding. What a tragic tale! How strange that Granma should tell me this the following evening. Although I didn't tell her what happened to me, I had a feeling that maybe Bob had been again in Spirit to visit her .... and had gone to the wrong room and found me instead! Well, whatever the case it just shows that he still loved her and wanted her. He was letting us both know that he was there.

(This is what so many people do not realise. Our loved ones haven't *died,* but live on in Spirit and are there for us. All we have to do is just "put a few thoughts out" and believe that they're there with us. But if we say, 'If you're about, where are you then?' they'll think, 'Oh, I've had enough of this .... I'm off!' Don't ever doubt the existence of Spirit. There's enough proof about. Once we accept and believe that they're still around, then they'll help us. It's as though we're driving along a road and they're sitting on top of a building. They can see just a little more than we can of what's around the corner.

They've also got a great sense of humour. They quite enjoy jokes such as, "Why did the Spirit Medium cross the road?" "So she could get to the Other Side.")

I felt for both Granma and Bob. Such a sad story. Yet it has a happy ending, to think that Bob came to her. Now that Granma's in Spirit, I know they're together again.

(There's a twist to the tale as well. I was being "used" in a relationship at that time and was going through a tough patch. Even today I won't utter the name of that person. It's sad to find out that someone's married after you've given your heart and your soul to them spiritually and physically. Yet every experience that I had and was to have was for a reason. So that I was to find the right words to say to those who need help. So that my heart would know just how others feel. And Spirit knows and understands. And will make themselves known to us in some way or another to comfort us in our dark night of the soul ....)

Well, Mother. I've got a great feeling deep inside me. I know something really exciting is about to happen. Somehow I've got to make you really proud of me. As soon as I know, I'll do it. I feel that I've got a great learning experience ahead of me. I keep hearing a man's voice from Spirit and he's telling me "Wait", so I'll wait. I feel that this time next year, New Year's Day 1996, will be a day of celebration. I wonder what it will be?

Happy New Year, Mother!

But God, I wish you were back!

Chapter Three

February, 1995

Dear Mother,

That's it! I know just what I'm going to do. I'm sending away for a hypnotherapy-psychoanalysis home correspondence course! It's terribly expensive, but if I get through the official exam I get seven letters after my name. In order to heal I feel it's what goes on up there (the mind) that has a physical bodily response. So many people who have had cancer and other serious illnesses, plus fears and phobias, have had stress in one way or another. It can be anger or sadness that people keep bottled up which eventually gets to them healthwise. If I can help people to get it all out of their subconscious minds, then physical ailments just won't stand a chance. I know I can do it. I believe in myself.

II

Dear Mother,

I'm worried about Steve. We've been to the hospital today. Apparently something's shown up. I've got to help him. Heal him. I know you can help me. Thanks for listening. Thanks for being with me now. Without him I just wouldn't want to carry on ....

III

Dear Mother,

My hypnotherapy course arrived this morning. I've never seen such a lot of notes in my life! It's snowing like mad now and I feel I've got the flu. Still, I must get on with it. Apparently some people get through to the final exam in two years. Others take as little as six weeks, depending on how much time one's got. Well, I'm not working right now so I've got all the time in the world!

Steve and I went to a Spiritual Healing exhibition the other day. I leaned up against the bar next to David Icke. He looked sad. He's done such a lot for Spirituality and yet people always quote him as saying that he was the "Son of God". Don't they realise the point he was trying to make is that we all are the sons of God? We all have the "God spark" within us. We're all born the same and we can all turn hate into love.

The love at that exhibition was truly amazing. Kind, happy faces and hugs all around. I've got into incense, too. There are that many types to choose from: rose, lavender, frankincense .... dozens and dozens. And besides smelling so nice they can really make you feel good and relax you. Going there with Steve has really made me feel that the world contains some beautiful people who truly care for the welfare of others and I just know that I really am on the right spiritual pathway.

IV

Dear Mother,

Well, thank you with all my heart! I did some hypnotherapy with Steve tonight (Sunday). Then some healing work — laying on of hands. When I did the hypnotherapy with him it was incredible. (Hypnotherapy is *not* to be confused with stage hypnosis. Hypnos comes from the Greek language and means "sleep". Basically, hypnotherapy is a "focalising of the mind". It is so safe to do and easy.)

I wrote down the hypnotherapy script especially for Steve. First time for both of us. At the end he opened his eyes (when told) and said, 'Have I been hypnotised?' I showed him my script — about fifteen pages long. His mouth fell open. 'I don't remember hearing any of it!' he said.

'No,' I replied. 'But your subconscious mind did and has stored it all just like a cassette. Besides, if you didn't hear a word why did you wake up when I told you to?'

Proof indeed!

Then onto the healing. Candles lit (I always light a candle for Spirit, signifying my love and thanks to them), incense burning, beautiful music in the background. A magical, spiritual atmosphere to say the least.

As I laid my hands on Steve I could feel your presence *very* near, Mother. It was as though your hands were on mine — drawing out all the pain, the negativity. (Now whenever I do spiritual healing I am often in a trance and many mediums tell me that it is the same with them.) Then I replaced all that negativity that I'd withdrawn with love and health. From you and Spirit to me and, through my hands, to Steve. It is an experience so beautiful it cannot be described on paper. But you were there, Mother.

After I had finished I sat on the carpet and looked at him. I can't remember my exact words, but they were something like, 'I know that you can't call a man beautiful, but you are, Steve. You look as though you have the face of an angel.'

And then, without any warning, *it* happened.

I had a large blue crystal ball on the coffee table next to a candle in a large holder. Suddenly the crystal ball threw itself *over* the candle and across the room where it crashed down to the floor! (This has never happened with anyone else since, so don't be put off!)

I knew it was you, Mother, giving me a sign that you really had been present all the way through the healing we did. Steve, of course, was really spooked out and sat on the settee with his mouth wide open. You could have driven a truck through it! I sat back and said, 'Thanks, Mother,' not at all shaken by the experience, but filled with feelings of love. It was as if you were saying, 'Well done, Ted.' It was at that moment that I *knew* I was going to be able to help people, especially with cancer. That very illness that you had had to endure for so long.

(While I write this, I have felt your hand on mine.)

You see, it's because I put my trust in Spirit. And in you, especially. I believe in you. I believe in me. I've not been given a gift that no one else has ever had before. But I've been given it because I believe in it.

And so, Mother, I've decided. Not only am I going to help rid people of pain, but remove the fear that's within their very heart. Because that's where it all begins, and very often it can be the *fear* of fear itself that causes so many problems. So to anyone reading this chapter: remove the fear, take out the swords from your hearts and start to love yourselves again.

V

March, 1995

Dear Mother,

Took Steve and his brother to their grandmother's funeral in Edinburgh today. We got stopped by a policeman, too! On the motorway! There was this plonker in a white car crawling along the third lane, a line of cars crawling along the inside lane and the middle lane was clear. 'Stuff this for a game of soldiers,' I thought and cruised along in the middle. THEN I realised why the inside lane was going so slowly. There was a police car in front! So he pulled me up and I had to get in the back of his car.

'What *exactly* do you think you were doing?' he said.

'Driving,' says I.

'Don't get clever with me! It was that guy's fault for hogging the fast lane at only 40 mph, but you shouldn't overtake on the left. Where are you going, anyway?'

'To take my friends to a funeral in Edinburgh.'

'Really? Let's hope it's not yours!' he snarled.

So out I got. Shame he was mad, 'cause I found him quite dishy. There's something about a man in uniform .... and the size of a truncheon .... that "gets me".

The funeral went well and I was proud to be there to support Steve, only .... well, Steve nearly didn't get there. On the morning of the funeral there was a mad panic. Steve had *lost* his trousers!

An hour later they were found — in the road! Apparently they had slid off the hanger when he got out of the car. Now just imagine if a neighbour's alsatian had discovered them. They probably wouldn't have been found for years and could have ended up in Dalkeith!

You know, Mother, while the funeral went on I was aware of a lady in Spirit sitting beside Steve's grandfather. It was his wife, of course. She didn't want to miss the service. After all, it was *her* funeral!

(When I go it's got to be like something out of a Hollywood film. I've got to be looking immaculate and dressed in white. And then .... Halfway through the service a beautiful lady wearing a large hat and veil so that no one can see who she is steps out of a black-windowed limousine, makes a dramatic entrance into the church and throws herself onto the coffin sobbing, 'No! No!' to the amazement of everyone. And then she leaves just as dramatically, with everyone wondering, 'Who *was* she?')

VI

March, 1995

Dear Mother,
Got the results of my first hypnotherapy test paper today. Excellent! was the remark at the bottom. I feel really happy about it and I do so want to make you proud of me. I've started a business course and met a beautiful new friend called Gabriela Leonowicz.

Gabriela made me feel good about myself. She brought out the beauty within me. She believed in me and what I was all about. We were certainly meant to meet: twin souls. Gabriela is an After Dinner Speaker, poet and author of the book "Poems for Big Kids", a book written while she lay flat on her back in excruciating pain following a back accident. Like me, she turned every bad thing in life around to her advantage. Obstacles become hurdles that we all get over if we make decisions and move forward with faith. Gabriela made me feel happy again. We became like brother and sister. She told me (and still tells me) how fabulous I was and with her I truly learned to laugh again. She could see that I had "star quality" — she has it herself — and it was thanks to her informing the editors that I appeared in a full-colour page spread in the "Telegraph" magazine. She wrote and told them all about me. She too had appeared in the same magazine earlier that year.

Gabriela is beautiful inside and out. She is certainly one of the brightest stars ever to enter and shine in my life. One day we will have the "Gab and Ed" show on TV or radio. She will always be with me, even though we are both travelling along different pathways. She is more psychic than she thinks and I know that it is only a short space of time before one day she will be standing before an audience giving out "messages".

I shall always be there for Gabriela. She has given me self-esteem and self-worth. She makes me happy. I do wish her boyfriend John would marry her. At least I could go to the wedding and catch the bouquet! Gabriela bought me my kitten Grimoire for my birthday.

For someone like myself who spends all his time giving out love, happiness and energy, Gabriela certainly "makes the clown laugh".

She's my friend. I love her.

VII

March, 1995

Dear Mother,
Stood by your grave today, darling, and shed a tear for you. Oh, I do miss you lately! I open your wardrobe and see your clothes hanging there and can still smell the fragrance of your perfume on them. Sometimes I feel as though you're just on holiday and will one day return.

Got good marks again on my second test paper. I've been studying from 7 a.m. to 4 a.m. each day since the course arrived. No wonder I'm getting depressed lately. I certainly need some rest!

An amazing thing happened while I lay on your bed today (Sunday). "That man from over the back" stood and stared right down the garden, as nosey as you like. Janet next door told me he'd been ill. Looks like it. Can't miss a thing, but if it makes him happy ....

VIII

(Monday)

Dear Mother,
Told Janet about the man today. 'I don't think you saw him,' she said. 'The funeral was two weeks ago ....' Amazing! Gone to Spirit and still doing what he loves best!

I'm beginning to see lots of people in Spirit lately, more than ever before. And if anyone wants to know about what happens when their pet passes over — well, it's exactly that. The times I've seen a dog or cat in Spirit while I'm driving along is nobody's business. Yes, there is a doggy heaven!

My dreams are certainly something to write home about right now. Everything I'm dreaming about is coming true. I've started dreaming a lot about people I've never met and then .... Two days later I find I'm standing right next to them in the supermarket. (While I write this I have a message coming through for an elderly lady called Dolcie. Now whoever Dolcie is — grey hair, glasses, walking stick — I shall probably meet her for the first time tomorrow in the post office. Isn't life exciting?)

I seem to be on great "highs" and then sudden "lows" for no apparent reason, unless it's because I miss you, Mother. Yet the more depressed I feel, the more my dreams are coming true. Still, I'm what's known as a "sensitive" and you become sensitive to vibrations around you all the while. That's why it is so easy to "pick" up on people when you're psychic. The more sensitive a person you are the more you open yourself up to all sorts of things. This is why it's important to close down at night. (More about this later in the book.)

Here's a good tip for anyone who wants to develop their psychic ability:

Write down the last thing that springs into your thoughts before you go to sleep. You may suddenly think, 'What? Crisps? Wolverhampton?' Well, write it down and in about three weeks' time, when you're sitting in the middle of Wolverhampton tucking into your bag of Smokey Bacon, it will dawn on you and you'll think, 'Gosh! I predicted this!' Try it and see ....

I've got to really push on now, Mother, and get through this course. I'm so glad I've met Gabriela. Jess, who was good to me when you passed over, has gone to live in Brighton. And Steve .... Well, I can't depend on him to always be there for me when I need him. After all, he has got his own life. Spiritually I feel very protected, but as far as friends go — they're all so busy and I've got to understand that.

I suppose I'm lonely.

I've got to shake off these "down" feelings! All the same, having them makes me realise just how important hypnotherapy is and how many depressed people I will be able to help because I'll know how they feel.

IX

Sunday, April, 1995

Dear Mother,

I've reached an all-time low. I've just spent all weekend thinking, 'What's the point?' Haven't washed. Haven't shaved. Haven't anything. Only smoked. Not eaten. Been over-doing it with my course. Still, sent off the final exam paper, so we'll see. I've exhausted my batteries and can't seem to recharge them.

Oh, Mother! I just don't want to carry on without you. I know that if I take my own life, I'll carry the "can't cope" feelings over into the next world and we may not even meet. But I can't go on like this! Money's short. Someone named Jock who I haven't seen for a while phoned on Sunday evening.

'You sound down,' he said. 'Do you want me to come over?'

'I don't care whether you do or don't.'

'Well, I'm coming over.'

I was even more upset by his visit.

'You need to widen your circle of friends,' he said.

Didn't I know it!

'I'm o.k.,' he continued. 'I've got my girl friend, my mum, dad, grandparents. Who've you go to turn to?'

By that point I was crying because he was right.

'*Who?*'

No one. I just want you, Mother. Jock didn't mean any harm and I know he felt bad about putting it that way, but he was right. You were always there for me, Mother. Always. I haven't felt your presence lately.

Have you deserted me, too?

I need you more than ever.

(This is one thing we *all* have to learn. When we need our loves ones in Spirit to help us, all we have to do is "talk" to them as though they are with us (and they are, always!) and then — this is extremely important — ask them what we can do for them in return. It's just the same as with friendships in life. It's got to be fifty-fifty. Also, it's no use saying, 'If you're there, *where* are you?' It's the doubts that make them think, 'Oh, they're doubting, so I'm off!' Today I'm never so happy as to be alone, chatting with Spirit and asking what they would like me to do for them in return for helping me. Turn the negative into the positive. Put out love to Spirit and never doubt that they can help us. That way we grow in love for Spirit and ourselves.)

Jock left. Oh, well. I'll get by somehow. Tonight I don't care if I live or die. I hope I die.

Chapter Four

Monday, April, 1995

Dear Mother, and ....

GOOD MORNING, WORLD! It's me and I'm staying!

Last night as I sat up in bed I felt a hand from Spirit rest upon my shoulder. It was so beautiful. Slept like a log, too. See! I *said* I felt you were looking after me. That comforting hand made me feel that you were there, as much as to say, 'There, there, it'll be all right.'

Got about fifty quid to my name, but I'll get by. Postman came .... phone bill, £100! I think I'll have to get my act together — QUICKLY!

It just won't do, this feeling negative. I've decided I'm going to be a man with a mission. A mission to make the whole world smile and to give sad people across the globe hope for the future and zest for life. So I'll start smiling first!

I believe in hugging. I hug someone at least five times a day. That way you give loving healing energy and you also receive it in return. You know how it feels if you're feeling down and someone takes you by the hand? You feel better instantly! So by hugging you are recharging someone's aura (the electro-magnetic field) with love.

I hugged my milkman Clive once (the one with the incredibly long life line) .... Haven't had any milk for weeks! You can sense who doesn't wish to be hugged. Also, I've learned from experience that it can get you into all *sorts* of trouble as some people can think you're "after them".

Hugging is a part of me now and it's wonderful to see sad people smile after you've hugged them. So .... everybody: START HUGGING NOW!

Went around to every Post office, village hall and notice board throughout Staffordshire and Shropshire today, advertising "Tarot Readings In Your Own Home".

(Never got any comeback, but at least I tried!)

I know I've got to use my psychic gifts. That's why we're blessed with them. If you want to become psychic for yourself, it won't happen. But if you want to develop it for the benefit of others it will happen and sooner than you anticipate.

I feel excited, Mother! As though a cloud has lifted. I've decided that I'm going to make the best of myself and not keep looking back.

You can't change the past, but you sure can change the future. Every day sees the chance to go out and touch someone's life. So to anyone who feels down and depressed I say: look forward! Look forward to the good things to come. Fear the worst and the worst will happen. Like attracts like. We've all been born the same, with the same amount of confidence, and we're all given a wonderful chance to make our world a better place. Think of the word LOVE. Now spell it back to front: EVOL. I know which I prefer! Life's too short to be sad and there's a big world out there waiting to be explored.

We have to keep reminding ourselves that we are special, each and every one of us. O.k. — we have many challenges to face, but they can be exciting challenges if we choose them to be. I feel that there's something exciting just around the corner, Mother!

KARMIC LAW

Many people ask me, 'Why am I having such an unhappy life? Why do so many people "take" from me? What have I done to deserve this?'

Let's assume that in a past life existence you were a user and a taker. Maybe a robber or thief, or even a murderer! Now, in this life, you are "paying back" the karmic debt. And you are paying the penalty.

So understanding that, let's imagine that you've already paid the price for all those things you ought not to have done. Now give love to everyone. Stop hating and feeling bitter. Don't judge. *Give.* Give to everyone you see. Give happiness. Stop judging yourself and accept the way life is. Be a giver, not a taker. Then you will find that life really will begin again. For the first time you will feel reborn and confident. Pay back to society what you may have taken from a past life and move forward. And remember, when life has a few downs, after the storms the rainbow of hope always shines through at the end.

Remove the karmic debt and in its place love everyone and everything of this life. And who knows ....? In the next life wonderful things *will* happen to you.

II

April, 1995

Dear Mother,

Oh, what wonderful news! I've got through the final exam of my hypnotherapy course with flying colours. I had to collect my two diplomas from the sorting office of the Royal Mail. There they were, with my full title: Francis Edward Ward, D.H.P., M.H.P.G. (Diploma in Hypnotherapy and Psychoanalysis, Member of the Hypnotherapy and Psychoanalysts' Guild).

I am so proud to be your son. If only you were here to celebrate with me! We could crack open a box of Earl Grey — just like we did when we had something to celebrate!

I want my name in lights for you, Mother, but something keeps telling me that you want my name in lights for *me.* What a joyous occasion! And no one here to celebrate it with me except me. *Now* I can get to work. Thanks for helping me to get through.

III

April, 1995

Dear Mother,

Have been doing healing work with Steve. Got to rid him of everything that's wrong with him. Have found, though, that everything I believe is right. Whatever goes on in the mind, bottled up, comes out in a physical way. He's been blaming himself a lot about the past and not telling anyone about his problems. Bit by bit he's telling me. Got to cure him mentally and physically once and for all. With you help, Mother. And also with God's.

IV

April, 1995

Dear Mother,

A new spiritual gift was given to me today. I was doing some healing with Steve, when I saw a light — just like the beam of a torch shining on his body. He opened his eyes.

'It's there, isn't it?' I asked.

'Yes, exactly,' he replied.

Then I knew that I had to concentrate with all my being on sending any illness away from that area. I was in trance and knew that there was someone with me in Spirit right by my side, helping me to channel all the loving healing energy I could for him. Then the light dimmed and went away.

This also is something that happens with spiritual healers. Spirit lights are sent to guide us so that we may know what part of the body needs healing. Other lights that many people see, often when sitting down during the day or evening, are known as 'watchers'. I do not like the term personally, but should anyone ever see a small light flicker on and off at any time, just rest assured that the lights are signs from people in Spirit letting us know that they are indeed watching over us. It's then that we need to communicate and welcome them into our homes. Don't be "spooked out". These people are obviously very close to us and are just making themselves known in a way so as not to frighten us. After welcoming them I usually light a pure white candle as an offering of pure love. Then I chat to them, telling them about my day or if there's anything bothering me and I ask what they would like me to do for them.

'Work for us and give us your love,' I have been told. Don't feel, by the way, that Spirit are with us every second. They do realise that we do have our personal moments! I also joke with Spirit a lot of the time. Did you hear the one about the two spirit mediums standing outside the library? There they were chatting, when another medium that they knew walked past. One of them said to her, 'Good day, dear.' No reply! She just kept on walking.

'How rude,' said the spirit medium. 'She just walked straight past and ignored us!'

'Ah, but she's depressed,' replied the other one. 'Haven't you heard the gossip? She's fallen into disrepute — she was caught having a bit on the "Other Side"!'

A lot of people smell fragrances associated with a loved one who has passed over. Perfumes, cigar smoke, flowers, books — just another way of making themselves known to us and that they're around.

Another wonderful thing happened during winter after I had attended a Spiritualist Church, Mother. I got back and found your bedroom lights on! (They do say 'leave a light on' when you go out, don't they? Nevertheless, what a welcome home!)

To go back to healing, we *all* possess healing energy. It's just the fact that not nearly enough people use it. Some are afraid because they don't understand what to do. Yet it's so simple. We are all surrounded with life-giving and healing energy. Just believe that person is *already* healed before you begin and you're halfway there. Because of the ability to see the human aura, if someone is sick there usually is a break in that aura. Once you see your first aura you will see them all the time. But someone I know has tried so hard to see it that he still can't. Why? He's trying too hard.

The first time it happened to me was many years ago. A lady was going absolutely mad about her sister. 'I hate her, I hate her, I HATE HER!' she screamed. Then I saw it: green, bright green. Green with envy, as they say. Ever since then I have been able to tell if someone's well, happy, ill, and more importantly — I can tell if someone's lying.

We all have the power to do the same!

V

May, 1995

Dear Mother,

Did a painting of Gabriela for her birthday. She was overwhelmed by it. Another psychic experience occurred.

'We need a frame for the painting,' she said.

'What about the one that fell off the wall?' asked her boy friend John.

Would you believe it? Only the night before, a framed mirror was found on the bathroom floor when Gabriela and John returned home.

It fitted the painting exactly! Even the colour of the frame — peppermint green — was a perfect match as it was so similar to the colour used in the background. Talk about coincidence .... I do love Gabriela. She is such a lovely person and we share many hours on the telephone giving each other support and friendship. She is someone who gives, and it's from the heart.

Thank you for guiding her to me, Mother.

Chapter Five

June, 1995

Dear Mother,

You should see the roses! So beautiful. The story *is* true. You are closer to God in a garden than anywhere else on earth. I always feel spiritual when I'm in the garden. It's so important to take time out to "smell the roses". Strange. I was cutting a beautiful rose for you for your bedroom, one of your favourite salmon pink ones, when I felt you were at the bedroom window, watching me!

I've been learning a lot about life lately and how important it is. There are so many sad people around that I know I can help them spiritually and mentally. I met a lady who had stomach cancer.

'I'm in so much pain,' she said. 'Can't sleep, can't lie down or even sit without feeling this awful pain.'

'Do you believe that I can help you?' I asked.

'I'll try anything!' was her reply.

'But do you believe that Spirit can really help to take the pain away?'

'Yes, I do, Ed. And I have faith in you.'

'Good,' I said. 'Let's get on with it.'

She sat in the armchair, full of pain. I burnt some lavender essential oil (to help calm down the nervous system). I put on some meditative music and then asked her to close her eyes. Before I knew it I was in trance, drawing out all the illness and replacing every bit of pain with love. Only when I felt it was right to finish did I stop. For a lady who admitted to not being able to sleep because of the pain, she did just that! Slept. Peacefully, like a baby. I sat down on the sofa and just waited, waiting for her to open her eyes in her own time.

Suddenly she opened her eyes, stretched and yawned. Then she gave out the loudest laugh I have ever heard in my life.

'You've cured me! It's GONE!' she yelled.

I sat and smiled, knowing that it wasn't *me* that cured her. I was just the catalyst.

I saw her for more healing work a couple of times after that. She didn't need it, but enjoyed the experience and the love and healing energy that I was able to transmit. Today she's well indeed and has phoned me many times, thanking me for her life.

That lady was one of the many to appreciate this and since then there have been many wonderful experiences, including two occasions of people having tests at hospitals where serious illness has been diagnosed, and have returned to the hospitals after spiritual healing to find that the illnesses have gone completely — which the specialists haven't been able to understand! Let me make it clear that I am not against orthodox medical treatment, but alternative spiritual healing really does work with or without medicine.

COLOUR THERAPY

Colour therapy is wonderful. The most healing colour of all is purple. If you ever feel drained or cannot sleep, or are in any pain the wearing of purple will alleviate symptoms quickly and effectively.
Green: superb for heart conditions, as its relaxing colour eases tension and stress. But it should not be used for people with cancer/tumours. Green is the colour of nature and makes things grow!
Pink: gives peace of mind and is the colour of love. It is good for women's complaints and breast disorders.
Orange: wonderful for clear thinking and intellect.
Silver: for clarity of mind and for peace. Also for feet problems, burning, etc.
Emerald green: for clairvoyance and heart conditions.
Blue: for healing and satisfaction. Also good for sickness/sore throats.
White: for cleansing the aura and for purity of mind and body.
Lilac: for sweet dreams and cancer.
Lavender: for headaches, sunburn, feeling sick.
Black: although termed a negative colour, it can also be a relaxant and many psychotherapists believe that if an insomniac imagines him/herself sinking into soft black velvet, that person will soon drift off to sleep.
Yellow: for happiness and general well being.
Red: for colds and flu.

So, for instance, when a person is feeling a little down: if they sit still and quiet (feet firmly on the floor and arms by their side), take three deep breaths, then close their eyes and imagine a beautiful yellow-gold translucent light that begins to glow behind their feet and slowly comes up right over the top of them and down to the ground, enveloping them in a golden psychic "shell" that keeps out negativity and gives them happiness, courage and lightness of spirit inside — then they cannot fail but feel happy again. If someone does this with belief for twenty minutes when needed, without doubt they will improve and the feeling will remain with them unless they choose otherwise.

Give it a go! As with anything in life, failing (as I tell many people) is not trying in the first place. We have to give life a go. Life with a capital L. I know of a lady who had just walked out of a twenty-year marriage and said that she had failed.

'But you've not,' I said. 'You *tried* for twenty years. You gave it a go!'

How can we achieve anything if we don't *try*? How can we reach our goals? How can we learn from our mistakes? "Mistake" is a strange word. I don't feel that we ever do make mistakes if we use our intuition and do what "feels so very right". So let's turn the word "mistake" into "barrier". We can be moving ahead quickly in life, when barriers come crashing down. Yet, however bad things seem, don't we always cross these barriers? Whenever we get through tremendous learning experiences, don't we become *stronger* mentally? And know that next time — if there is a next time — we will be so much wiser in our future actions.

It's how we look at life and what it throws at us that we can learn to accept and to change it for the better. We all learn to get through, somehow. Sometimes we have to learn how to walk away from associations that only have "motivation" behind their every move, which is something that I've learned the hard way. Once we've learned to give love and happiness to people — every day sees the chance to touch someone's life — all the right people do appear in your life and it shows that "what you sow, you reap".

It is so important for only *you* to have control over yourself. I have met so many people who have been controlled by someone and *it just won't do*! I've allowed it myself — and regretted it. So step number one is for you to:

1. Be the only one to have control over yourself.
2. Be honest with yourself and with everyone else.
3. Forgive yourself so that you can move forward.
4. Totally love yourself as a special and unique person before you start loving others.
5. Give without receiving. If someone is in your life who needs help, then give but never expect anyone to repay you. Give totally and completely. For example, if you help someone financially, just give if you're able to. By giving and not asking for repayment you free them from their shackles. If you give and want them to repay you, you have freed them from one thing and bound them to you.
6. Greet the day with sheer love, anticipation and appreciation for the gift of life.
7. Thank Spirit and God for your life, however humble. The best things are still free — beauty of nature and every blessing we have been given.
8. Don't give depression a chance. Close the door on it like an unwelcome visitor and put protection around you and your property. (And anyone else, for that matter.) "Keep in" love and happiness within your four walls and "keep out" negativity.
9. Look upon life as an exciting challenge.
10. Live life to the full.

I suppose you could call these "Mystic Ed's Ten Commandments"!

II

June 28th, 1995

Dear Mother,

Thirty-nine tomorrow, Mother! Going to Derbyshire tomorrow for the day. It's heatwave right now. Still doing my business course and enjoying being with people. Folk have nicknamed me Mystic Ed *again*. People have been calling me that for years now. It's only because of all the chains and rings and things I wear when I'm doing tarot readings. I'm really far too spiritual to be called that, but it's a fun name. Spirit gave me the name Aegir, but people insist on calling me Mystic Ed or Mystic for short. I like "Mystic". Adds a touch of mystery ....! Good name for a tarot reader.

TAROT AND TAROT READERS

Tarot comes from the Egyptian *Tar* and *Rot*, which means "Royal Road". Some fortune-tellers are genuine, some will tell you absolute garbage. I recall going to see someone in London years ago with two female friends from work. My friends watched from a distance.

'Your marriage isn't going very well, is it?' began Madame X.

'I'm not married,' says I.

'But you have been!'

'Er .... No.'

She'd obviously seen my friends (both blonde) waiting and insisted: 'I'm telling you that you *are* married and that you're going to have a *divorce*.'

'No, I'm not married!'

'Yes, you are .... to a blonde woman.'

'No, I'm not!'

'Yes, you *are*!' she shrieked.

'I am NOT!' I yelled back.

'My name is Madame .... and I've been reading the cards for fifty-five years. *Fifty-five years!* So don't lie to me.'

'O.k., o.k.,' I retorted. 'But I'm still not married.'

'Well, your ex-wife will come back into your life ....'

(Oh, God! Can't she get the message? I'm not even the marrying kind!)

Finally Madame X announces: 'You will star in an Italian film. You .... will .... become .... BEN HUR!'

Well, I know, other mediums know and the cards know that I shall appear one day in a film, but something tells me it won't be as Ben Hur. For a start, I haven't got Charlton Heston's chest — or his toupee. Nevertheless, I have got his autograph and Ben Hur *is* one of my favourite films, so she didn't get it *all* wrong.

'What can you see in your crystal ball?'

'Nothing. I forgot to bring it with me today!'

There are tarot readers and tarot readers. Some go by the little handbook that comes with a set of tarot cards. This serves the purpose well. There are 78 cards in a pack: 22 major cards and 56 minor cards. Some readers only use the major cards, but I've found that it can be like reading a book. You wouldn't only read half of it, would you? After a lot of practise, reading the cards becomes easier and the general meanings "stick"; yet with me and many other readers something else happens. I will turn over the cards, the original meanings are there and then something "clicks". Often I get names, dates, places, years, months — all types of things that are relevant to that particular "sitter". It's as though once I've turned over the cards it has turned the handle of a psychic door and opened it. One quite famous medium once told me that Spirit will never "come through" during a tarot reading. Well, I beg to differ. With me it does and very often. I can turn a few cards over and get, straight through my ears, the name of a deceased loved one without it's being in the meaning of the cards. Often after the name has come to me I will see that loved one standing by the sitter's side. Or smell a fragrance that the sitter associates with them.

I remember once turning over the cards for a lady I had never met before and I just came straight out with, 'Harry Spencer. And your maiden name was Conlon.' Then I "felt" Harry enter the room behind me. He went and stood right by the lady and placed his hand on her shoulder.

'Bifocal spectacles,' I said. 'He's wearing them now.'

That lady left in tears. Tears of joy. She wasn't looking for recognition from her husband, yet it was his choice to come along that evening.

Some people come purposefully for this sort of thing to happen and it doesn't.

That's where the word *medium* comes from. The clairvoyant is the medium, the channel by which Spirit can communicate.

(How did I know I was a medium? Because it says so on my underpants!)

Other times I can turn cards over (again, nothing like this in the actual meanings of the cards) and I will come out with:

'Your husband is driving a red metro. Has the exhaust pipe dropped off yet?'

'No ....'

'Well, he'd better get it checked out then.'

Next day arrives. Phone rings. A woman's voice says excitedly, 'You know about my hubby's exhaust pipe?'

'Mmmm....'

'Well, he marched into the house yesterday after you did me my reading and said "Did you hear *that*? Well, the bloody exhaust pipe's fallen off right in the drive!"'

So that's how a reading tends to work with me. Everything I "see" and say comes directly from the heart. I'm honest with people (or there's no point having a reading if you don't want the truth) and if I see a relationship is going nowhere I just have to say so! At least if a person *knows* (and their intuition has usually told them in the first place) one way or another, then they can move forward. I usually see a happy ending for most people and if someone is in tears when they first meet me, but at the end of the reading feels that they can greet life with hope and a good outcome to all they put into life, then I know I haven't failed.

People shudder when the "death" card shows up and yet 99% of the time it shows an end to an old cycle of their life with a new one to begin. It is very rare that it shows a potential death.

I must add that there's nothing spooky about tarot reading. It doesn't mean to say that I run around my bungalow at midnight, naked and holding a candle! It is *not* a black magic or witchcraft tool when used properly in the right hands. It is "future guidance" and you can even get people to pray, go to church and ask God for forgiveness through the cards. There is nothing to be afraid of, either using them or having a reading. If you use the cards with love and respect and do readings so that you can help people to "find their Way", then only good can happen.

That's a very important part of psychic and spiritual work. If you want to develop your gifts for *you*, nothing will happen. If you want to develop them for helping others, you will achieve so much. Your psychic ability will develop overnight and you *will* be able to help other people.

When choosing a set of cards, buy them yourself and see which deck you are drawn to. If someone buys them for you, you are likely to not like them as its their choice and not yours. Don't look at every card thinking, 'I'll never learn all this lot', but just learn the meanings to a few cards at a time and you'll find that with patience the general meanings will stick in your mind. When you do your first readings, speak your truth clearly and refer to your handbook if you get stuck. Again I repeat: go by your intuition, your gut feelings. If you feel you have to say something, then say it. Your intuition is telling you to say to that person what they are meant to hear. Then wait and see. You will find that if your words come from the heart, your predictions will come true.

One word of warning: never use any type of Spiritual tool for monetary gain. Because it is so selfish, it will have the opposite effect and money will be taken from you! The cards are meant to guide "spiritually".

III

June 29th, 1995

Dear Mother,

I'm thirty-nine, Mother, and you're not here. Makes me feel sad. My first birthday without you. At midnight last night I heard footsteps running to my front door. I knew whose footsteps they were — Gabriela's! What an "eve" to a birthday! I opened the front door in my dressing gown (what a funny place to put a door!) and in walked a handmade kimono and a bunch of roses from a lady who I not only admire, but am honoured to have as my friend. And then she left! You know, you're around *every* time Gabriela and I are together. I feel it. I sense it. Thank you for her.

Went to Dovedale with Steve on what must have been the hottest day of the year. Had a lovely day. Back early this evening. Steve had to see his mother before he flies off to Sweden for two weeks. Now I feel dreadfully alone and sad.

Oh, Mother — if you could visit me so I can see you, can't it be today on my birthday? I must remember that you have been called to Spirit to be "there" in the kingdom of love or else you would still be here physically. I'm being selfish, because you are now living your life in another dimension, on another plane. Sometimes I feel that I'm dreaming and one day I'll wake up and find you here. Sad, isn't it?

Yet I've got this absolutely electric feeling within me as though it's "not long now". The cards tell me that I'm going to meet someone in TV or on radio born under the birthsign of Gemini. Gabriela's a Gemini, but it's not her. This is someone I've yet to meet. Isn't life exciting!

IV

July, 1995

Dear Mother,

Got myself a telephone-answering machine today. It says to put on it, 'Please leave your name, number and message after the tone'. You can forget that for a start! People keep saying to me about life, 'I'm looking for the happy medium' and I reply, 'Well, you've found him, haven't you?' So, message number one:

You're through to Mystic Ed, the Happy Medium. As I don't foresee anything in the future, leave your name, number and message after the tone and as soon as the mists begin to clear I'll phone you back .... er .... er .... What can I end it with?

I know! I've got it, Mother! It's gonna be my catchphrase and message to the millions:

ENJOY YOUR LIFE AND SMILE!

(Received my first message from Steve on the way from Sweden. That's got to be a world first!)

So, Mother, I've got the message. Image is the thing, let's all work on a unique personal image, the way we look, act and behave.

I've decided. I may be a serious fully qualified hypnotherapist and healer, but I'm also Mystic Ed, the Happy Medium.

The auburn hair is going to get redder. I'm busy creating my own style. I want to be *me* and not model myself on anyone else. If anyone *dares* copy me, I'll change it. If anyone doesn't like the red hair, it will get redder! As long as we all remember to let the beauty and the love shine through .... that's what counts! Gazing at myself in the hall mirror, I turned to look at the portrait in oils I did of you many, many years ago.

'I want my name in lights for you, Mother,' I said aloud.

The painting moved and was all "to cock". It was as if you were saying, 'But I want *our* name in lights for *you*.'

I stood back and smiled knowingly. Each time I say something to you, your painting moves.

'O.k., o.k.,' I continued. 'What are you up to, Mother? I have a feeling that you're waving your magic wand for me. Can't *wait* to see what's going to happen.'

'I'm going to have my own radio or TV show one day soon,' I've said to people.

'Oh, sure. And I'm the Prime Minister,' they've replied.

Probably has sounded like a big dream that I'm obsessed with. But I'm not. I "know". Can't think how it will happen! Yet Gabriela believes it. And Steve believes it.

Why *not* me? I've been asking myself. I know that if ever I did have a chance for radio or TV, that I would be different from all the rest. Not modelled on anyone. Just me and my ideas, so that others may find their way.

Chapter Six

July, 1995

Dear Mother,

I had a dream last night, Mother, about something I want to obtain before I die. A Paradise anyone in the world can come to whether they are rich, poor, famous or otherwise. A place in a warm climate with a paradise garden overlooking the sea where anyone who is depressed, alone, or even terminally ill with cancer or AIDS can come to. Where they can find healing, happiness and love. Where they can come to feel renewed, to be given peace of mind, body and spirit; where they can feel re-born and confident. Then they can go back to their lives with hope in their hearts as well as love; if terminally ill, they will have found great courage and dignity without fear. This service is to be absolutely free of charge. Age, colour or creed will make no difference.

To get this dream fulfilled I will have to become mega-rich, but I know one day it will happen. Somehow.

In my dream last night I was with Elizabeth Taylor and we were standing side by side on top of a hillside, with beautiful flowers all around us and we were looking out at the ocean. She was Elizabeth, the psychic lady; Elizabeth, the woman who has feelings. I said to her, 'He's coming back, please don't worry. I'm here to protect you.' (It was announced a few days later that Elizabeth and Larry Fortenski had separated!) She was dressed simply in dark leggings and a top. She is so underestimated and hounded by the press, I wish they would leave her alone. There is far more to this lady than meets the eye. She is sensitive, kind, loving and, as I said before, very psychic. It takes one to know one!

So one day it will happen: my paradise and Elizabeth will be there. The money will surely have to come by way of donation, but when it is meant to be it will be. After all, Elizabeth does do a great deal of heartfelt work for AIDS.

One day my dream will come true.

As for our dreams ....

Dream interpretations can often be difficult, yet often so very easy to decipher. Speaking now as a fully qualified hypnotherapist, we must remember that a lot of the stresses that build up during the day are released at night through our dreams. With that in mind, be pleased instead of being disturbed if you have nightmares.

Make notes of *all* your dreams. Keep a special dream diary beside your bed and when you wake up in the night with a dream buzzing through your mind, don't think, 'I'll write it down in the morning'. By morning you'll have forgotten what it was! Force yourself awake and jot it down, simply but to the point. Get a dream interpretation book and look up each stage of the dream. A lot of dreams are symbolic. Often our most psychic premonitions are given through our dreams, so it is very important that we write everything down. Ninety-nine percent of my dreams do come true. Writing all of them down in a special book helps me to keep a record of them. For instance, if names, places or months come into your dreams and you record them, you may find that when something happens days, weeks or months later you'll think, 'Gosh! I dreamt about this! I predicted that this would happen'.

Therefore you are already on the right road to becoming a psychic. If you have regularly recurrent dreams, you really need to analyse them properly or even go to see a reputable hypnotherapist to take you back and discover just why you are having them. Obviously something is worrying you that consciously you are unaware of and this worry is deep-rooted in your subconscious mind. It could be that right at the back of your mind you have kept an incident that really bothered you when you were a child.

Persistent bad dreams can be eased by the simple step of placing a piece of amethyst under your pillow. I would suggest this to anyone, as an amethyst helps naturally to give restful sleep and peaceful sweet dreams.

(When I was a child of six I would dream about someone whom I had never met. A day or two later, walking through town holding Mummy's hand we would suddenly bump into *that* person!)

Use your dreams wisely and remember the old saying, 'If you dream something more than once it shall surely come true'. Especially if you dream about true love! I can remember vividly dreaming about a road and a church that I had never seen before. Three weeks later I was walking along and there I was — in that same road and looking at that very church! It's premonitions like these that prove to you that dreams can be a real help in discovering your underlying psychic self.

II

July 20th, 1995

Dear Mother,

Saw the most wonderful aura drift around the cherry tree today. Every living thing has a life force energy around it. It was a beautiful sight, but I felt sorry for the tree. It's been so hot and dry for weeks now. No rain at all. It was as if the life-force energy was coming up from the ground, literally searching for moisture.

Went to a "mysterious crop circle" meeting tonight in Shropshire. Met there two wonderful new friends that I sat next to — Brian and Susan. Thoroughly enjoyed the meeting, but had a fit of the titters as usual. Everyone except Brian and Susan were all *so* serious. I felt I want to shout out, 'Has the cat died?'

Or more appropriately, 'Is anybody there? One knock for yes, two knocks for no!'

Am looking forward to hearing Gabriela on BBC Radio WM on Sunday on the Rustie Lee Show.

Now more about:

BRIAN AND SUSAN

'I'm a hypnotherapist. Would you like a leaflet?' I said to the charming gentleman beside me at the crop circle meeting.

'*Laverly!* I'm a hypnotherapist. Would you like a card?!'

So that's how we met. Those wonderful people — so wonderful that love literally shines from them and touches everyone that they meet. (Shame about my leaflets. Had about 500 printed and didn't get a single phone call. Why? *I forgot to put my phone number on!!*)

With Brian and myself to help people, anyone who goes to see a psychiatrist ought to get their heads examined!

Our friendship was definitely meant to be and it was later on, after appearing on radio, that we really hit it off in a big way.

I've nicknamed Brian the "Mad Monk of Muxton" for no particular reason except that he lives there and it rhymes. Named Susan the "Pussy Fairy" for a very obvious reason: her love of cats. They have four!

Since our meeting Brian has become like a brother, father and best friend to me. He has an auric beauty that surrounds him and he is very protected by Spirit. I often worry about people using him or putting on him, as he is one of life's givers and gives love to everyone. Sue, his wife, is the same. Neither of them judge or have a harsh word to say about anyone. Sue is loving kindness itself and has got a wicked sense of humour that gets anyone rolling around on the mat with mirth! They have given me so much and I've given them so little. They are just happy to see me get on in life and for me to be their friend, which I always will. Their kindness and generosity bowl me over and I could cry with pride in having such special friends.

When you walk into their home it's like coming home — yet like coming home to a Doris Day and Rock Hudson movie. Tea is always on the table and coffee on the boil. They, like Gabriela, *believe* in me. I owe a great deal to them for what kindness and love they have given to me and yet they don't wish me to do anything in return. Maybe they have found the secret of love. Giving. Spiritually, Mother, I know that they were sent to me like Gabriela was because all you ever really cared about was that should anything ever happen to you I wouldn't be lonely.

Bri and Sue are extremely gifted psychically and spiritually. I owe a great deal to them for helping me in many psychic matters like "closing down" and psychic protection, and protecting myself against harmful influences. I am always welcome there and together we have enjoyed many spiritual adventures. All they ask is for me to be happy and I know I make them happy too.

Should I ever become rich I will give them my last penny (although knowing them, they wouldn't accept it!) so they can have their heart's desire: a one-way ticket to the island of Malta and enough money so they could buy their dream home there: it is their special island that they love so much. Together we share lots of laughter, sometimes a few tears. They are there for me and I thank God for them. Brian is a brilliant hypnotherapist and Sue helps to trace family trees — adoptions a specialty. Spare-time hobbies they enjoy doing and that help a lot of people.

Brian and Sue are angels from Heaven and I hold a special place of love for them deep within my heart. LOVE = BRIAN + SUSAN!

HYPNOTHERAPY

Hypnotherapy is a *therapy* and not to be confused with stage hypnosis. Hypnos comes from the Greek word meaning sleep. Basically, hypnosis is a focusing of the mind. Many people say, 'I don't think that I could be hypnotised,' and I usually reply, 'But you go to sleep, don't you?'

How many things can be helped and cured naturally and safely with hypnotherapy? Depression, anxiety, sleeplessness, confidence, smoking cessation, weight control, fears, phobias, nervousness, bad habits, stress, temperament problems .... The list goes on and on.

There is meditative therapy and positive suggestion therapy. Sometimes it is necessary to take a client back to their childhood days, as very often that can be where a problems begins. Once the emotion has been released (known as the catharsis) during hypnosis, then the client can move forward in life without having that fear or phobia as a problem because they now realise the originating cause. You are taken down (under) in hypnotherapy gently and quietly and brought out of hypnosis the same way. Afterwards you feel calm, relaxed and confident.

PAST LIFE REGRESSION

Sometimes a person is taken back to a previous life either a) because of their interest in the subject and really feeling that they *have* lived before, or b) because there may be a problem that could have been caused by something that happened in the last life or even lives before it.

Some people have gone back as many as four or five lives. Others haven't had a past life and this is their first, in which case they may describe their birth into this world.

Past lives is a fascinating subject and many problems of today can be solved by "going back", therefore enabling the person to realise why he/she may be having problems now.

Some people describing their past life (or lives) under hypnosis find that they were very simple people leading quite ordinary lives. Others reveal what an important life they once had. Don't forget that a man today could have been a woman in a former life and vice versa. I know of a lady who has been a man in every one of her five former lifetimes, yet she is the most feminine and ladylike person you could wish to meet.

I myself had to be something out of the ordinary! I went way, way back in time to the land of Ancient Egypt and discovered that I was the Spirit-guide of an Egyptian Princess, the mother of Tutankhamen. I would very much like to go back again to know who I was before being a Spirit-guide. Naturally, most people would like to go back and find that they had been someone famous like Henry the Eighth, Cleopatra or Elizabeth the First. So it's more than a bit disappointing to find our how ordinary they were.

An example of past life regression is that of a lady who came to see me for a feature to be written in a local newspaper.

'Sarah,' she muttered. 'Sarah James.'

In her past life she turned out to have been a young woman in Herefordshire. She had a maid and she recollected how she had lost her father. She wore brown lace-up boots, simple country clothes and a large hat complete with feathers and a hatpin. Back in this life, she did some research and found her birth records dated 1872 in the Parish Church in Herefordshire. She was the only Sarah James recorded.

Another occasion was another young lady who went back to Marlborough in the 1850s. She was leaving home to find true love — and found it. (She did this in this life too.) Later on she went to Marlborough and found the same house where she had once lived all those years ago. Although very shabby, it still had the same colour front door and was still surrounded by the same trees and cornfields.

Future Regression is becoming something of an interest nowadays and one person described their retirement home in Devon. They now live in that very house in Devon that they described under hypnosis.

It can be fascinating to retrace your past life regression experience by visiting areas you describe under hypnosis. You could even trace your family tree and see what fun and interest you have doing it.

Hypnotherapy is safe, enjoyable and beneficial to everyone. You just close your eyes and let your mind drift and dream .... drift .... and .... dream .... and remember! What goes on in the mind has a physical bodily response, so what better therapy than hypnotherapy! To calm, to relax and to become a more self-confident, self-assured and positive person as the result!

III

July, 1995

Dear Mother,

Heard Gabriela on the Rustie Lee Show on Radio WM today. It was the best and funniest interview I've ever heard on radio. Yet Gabriela is far too beautiful to be on radio. She needs the world to see her on TV. On radio Gabby sounded confident, radiant and certainly gives it her best shot. Her book has been published: "Poems for Big Kids". I think it will sell well. She's put a lot of effort and expense into printing it, so she deserves to get on in every way.

You know, Mother, I haven't felt at all down lately. Instead, I feel excited. I *know* something really great is going to happen really soon. As though I've just got to turn the key in a door and unlock it and step out into something wonderful. The cards keep telling me I'll be famous. I know I'll have my own TV or radio show. The more I've gone out into the world and tried to touch someone's life with love and happiness, the more I feel contented. Life's going to get better and at the moment all my dreams are coming true, all of them.

I've started to feel the presence of a gentleman in Spirit around me. Younger than myself and sometimes I see an auric light around the handle of the living room door. It's then when I mentally invite him in to join me. The light around the door disappears and I feel his presence very strongly as he stands by my side. To date I've not "seen" him, but know when he's around. I often smell his tobacco. One day a medium came to have a cup of tea with me and she suddenly came out with, 'I've just seen a gentleman walking down your hallway.' It's strange that I haven't actually seen him myself. He will make himself known to me when he chooses. I've felt him touch my hand and once he laid his hand on my shoulder. It's comforting. I love him for being close to me.

This type of thing mustn't "spook out" people if it happens to them. All folk must do is remember that Spirit love us and will protect us *if* we continue to try and do the right thing. I do enjoy having my friend in Spirit about the house. I know when he's around (while I write this I know that he has just sat on the settee to the left of me and is peering over my arm, trying to see what I've written about him). Just remember that if anyone ever sees any small lights flicker on and off — not electric ones — but small blue or gold ones, that they are Spirit lights and are obviously fond of us. It's their way of making us realise without frightening us that they are close by.

IV

July 27th, 1995

Dear Mother,

'Was talking to Rustie Lee after the show and we were comparing our bad backs,' said Gabriela on the telephone. 'Do you want the phone number to Radio WM? Maybe you could have a chat.'

'Could do, Gabby. Maybe I could discuss healing with her.'

Gabriela gave me the number. A strange, exciting feeling went through me. I recalled many years ago watching Rustie on TV and saying to you, Mother, how I knew one day I would meet her. You said, 'Yes, I know you will, dear.' So if I *did* talk to Rustie on the telephone — that's if they put me through to her — my prediction will come partly true.

It's Friday, July 27th, 1:30 p.m. Phoned BBC Radio WM from an upstairs room in an office where I was getting some photocopies.

Ring. Ring.

'Hello.'

'Can I speak to Rustie Lee, please?'

'Speaking.'

(Gosh! I've got right through!)

'This is Mystic Ed ....'

'Ha ha haagh! Mystic .... *who?*'

'Mystic Ed, the Happy Medium.'

'Happy Medium .... Ha ha haagh! Do you know, that's really strange. I'm not always here at this time.'

We chatted away as though we'd known each other for years and suddenly, after talking about Spirituality and tarot readings, she said, 'What are you doing on Sunday?'

'Er .... nothing in particular, Rustie.'

'Good! How do you fancy being a guest on my show?'

'Sounds good. What'll I be talking about?'

'Everything you're into, darling. Don't worry .... Just come along and be yourself!'

After putting the receiver down I am filled with excitement. WOW! I'm going on BBC radio! I can't believe it and yet I can because it's just happened. I knew something out of this world was going to happen. Driving back home on a very hot day, I'm driving like a maniac! I'm so excited and how I didn't crash into anyone or end up in a field by accident I shall never know.

But I got home safely and walked into the front room. 'Oh, hello!' I thought. My beautiful blue crystal ball, the one that jumped over the candle after I had been doing healing with Steve, was now near the door by the hallway! While I was out the ball had moved from the coffee table to where I found it — about twelve feet away.

'Thank you, Mother! Thanks again for making magic in my life. And for the sign. I'm going to give it my best shot on Sunday, although I'll probably be on for ten minutes, a quarter of an hour at most. But I'll give it my best shot for *you,* Mother. Thank you.'

That evening is spent thinking, 'What *shall* I say? What shall I wear? Oh, I must phone everyone and tell them ....!'

'I'll take you, my darling Ed,' says Gabriela. 'I know the way and at least you can just sit in the passenger seat and stay calm.'

Isn't it exciting ....?

V

July 29th, 1995

Dear Mother,

I'm sitting in bed, writing this to you and gazing again at your photo. From black and white to colour, revealing your beautiful auburn hair.

Guess what's been happening today? I've been on BBC Radio WM and met a new friend we both knew I would meet: Rustie! My ten minutes turned into two hours and I stayed on throughout the show.

It started when I was getting ready to leave at mid-day.

Like an angel dressed in white — white shoes, trousers and shirt, suntan just so, hair red and shining, immaculate. I've got to say it! I've never felt or looked so good. May sound terribly big-headed, but it's true. I feel good about *me*. One more look in the mirror ....

'Say break a leg, Janet,' I call over the fence to my lovely neighbour with a heart of gold — a lady who will help anyone.

'Break a leg, duck,' she calls back in her charming Hampshire accent.

Popped over to Steve's on my way to Gabriela's.

'I'm supposed to be going to a barbecue this afternoon with my girl friend, but I'll stay home and record it for you,' he said.

I arrive at Gabriela's place. Off we go and reach BBC Pebble Mill Studios at about twenty to two.

'You're very calm, Ed,' said Gabriela.

'I know. I don't feel nervous. Not one little bit.'

Well, I never .... I'm just about to have cigarette before we go in and then Rustie drives up. Fag gets whizzed under the car! Rustie looks at me, I look at her. She knows who I am without even having to say anything. She kisses me on the cheek and we have a hug. She says my hair looks beautiful. With her is her fiancé and manager Andreas and Rustie's son James. What wonderful people! I can tell Rustie's psychic. Love just shines and radiates outwards from her face.

'Let's go in. We'll go through what we'll talk about.'

The show goes really well. We talk about my beliefs in healing, hypnotherapy and predicting.

'Would you like it if we open up the lines so people can phone in to you, Mystic?'

'Super!'

The phone lines are jammed.

What a wonderful day! I've become a "name". Gabriela and I drive back along the M6. To everyone who overtakes us we yell out, 'Excuse me, don't you know we're celebrities?'

It's a wonderful feeling and a lovely warm glow radiates inside us both.

'Two hours, Ed. You were on for TWO HOURS!'

Some people try all their lives to get on radio for two minutes. In my case it was obviously meant to be.

I get back home to find my answering machine full of messages. Some were really ridiculous, like, 'Hello, my name's Judy and I'm a Leo. Thank you.' (No number left. I think people thought that my home number was left as a continuation of the tarot phone-in — at my expense.)

At least six calls were from various people who just phoned to say things like,

'Heard the show today, Mystic, and just phoned to say how happy I feel. More confident and optimistic. (Shouldn't that be *optimystic*?) You've done me a power of good.'

Some calls just said, 'Thank you, Mystic Ed.'

One call set my heart racing like mad for at least two seconds.

'Heard the show today, Mystic, and were very impressed. We want to get you on GMTV asap. Please phone us at your earliest convenience. The number is 01543 ....'

There I am scribbling it down when I think, 'Hello — that's a Cannock number .... It's Steve .... having me on!'

I phone him back.

'You certainly had me fooled,' I said.

'What a *Star*!' he exclaimed.

'Really? Was it o.k.?'

'O.k.? It was fantastic! Got it all on tape. I'll be round with it so you can listen to it .... and a bottle of champagne.'

Steve comes round, bottle in hand.

'What a *Star*!' he says again.

Champagne to celebrate, but we didn't have a bottle opener!

'Oh, Steve, only a few short months ago and I didn't want to live. And now this!'

It was wonderful to share the moment with him.

Oh, Mother, what a wonderful day. Thank you again. It's been just like a dream, a wonderful dream. They're going to do a feature in the Lichfield, Cannock and Rugeley Mercury next week. Apparently the photographers are coming too!

Whatever next?

Chapter Seven

July, 1995

Dear Mother,

I've got two feelings. One is that something else great is going to happen — but also a feeling that something awful is going to happen. Soon. It's as though the angel of death has passed by my door and I know that I'm going to need all my health and strength to get through it. Yet I know I will get through what's coming. I must go by my intuition and if anything feels wrong — it will be. I mustn't miss the signpost that will guide me away from what will happen.

Had another funny experience on my way to the Mercury offices in Cannock today. Couldn't find a place to park, only half on and half off double yellow lines. Maybe just for a few minutes ....? And then She appeared! The black and yellow striped parking vulture. I look out of the open window of the car. She looms over me.

'Oh, what a *beautiful* smile,' I say in my most flattering voice. 'You do look gorgeous — is it your birthday?' I beam hopefully at the vulture. 'Er .... I don't suppose I can park here for a couple of minutes? Oh, you *do* have a beautiful smile!'

'O.k., go on!' she says. 'But be quick!'

And off she went, really smiling. Although it was done in a very motivating way, I did her some good by making her feel *good* about herself.

(I've been parking on double yellow lines ever since!)

It doesn't take a minute to make someone's day.

That week was a busy one, wasn't it, Mother? Three newspapers have interviewed me and taken photos. They're calling me "Cannock's psychic celebrity".

I've now got an image and I'm going to continue to create my own style. Different, unlike any other psychic, astrologer or clairvoyant. O.k., so Mystic Ed is very gimmicky — but he's getting noticed.

'You don't expect anyone to take you seriously with a name like *that,* do you?' a reporter asked.

'It's strange,' I replied. 'But people do, you know. It makes them smile and when I say I'm the "Happy Medium who's got the largest and shiniest crystal balls in the business" they always laugh. What better healing is there than laughter? When people meet me I not only cheer them up and make them laugh with my definitely offbeat and rather risqué sense of humour, but they get to know the real me. The "human" Mystic Ed who talks from the heart. So, yes, I do and am continuing to touch people's lives in my own individual style. I am very spiritually-minded, but I think I've found the key to reaching out to people. Make 'em laugh. Sometimes we have to look long and hard at ourselves in the mirror, laugh and think, "Prat!". Laugh it off and start again.'

This brings to mind another joke:

I got to thinking about one famous lady, who whenever you see paintings of her always looks so sad. I mean Mary, the Mother of Jesus. So I thought, 'I've had enough of this.' I jumped onto the nearest 747 and zoomed off to Heaven for the day. There she was, standing outside the pearly gates with the baby Jesus in her arms and still looking completely fed up.

'Oh, Mary,' I said. 'You're the most famous lady in the whole world, with the most famous son in the whole world. But why do you always look so sad?'

Mary looked up at me with her sad eyes, down at Jesus and then back up at me again. She sighed deeply and said, 'We were hoping for a *girl.*'

II

August, 1995

Dear Mother,

Since the newspaper features I've certainly become known everywhere I go.

'It's him! It's that man .... Look!' they say.

I go into the post office for a stamp and people in the queue start turning around and looking. It's funny, exciting and embarrassing all at the same time.

'It *is* him! Told you! It's that man out of the papers .... The one that we heard on Rustie's radio show.'

'Can I have your autograph?' asked a lady in the Safeway and I autographed her till receipt!

They said, 'Are you Gary Glitter's brother?'

(Something to do with the way I raise my left eyebrow.)

'Lionel Blair's?'

'Cliff Richard's?'

'Dr Hilary Jones?'

'You've *got* to be related to David Essex!'

One lady came up to me in a garden centre and shrieked, 'It's *you*, isn't it?'

I wanted to say, 'Who did you expect? Batman?'

Another lady dared to cross my threshold and said, 'You look old for thirty-two.'

'That's because I'm thirty-nine.'

'GOD! You look old for thirty-nine!' And she went on to say that she hadn't got any friends and didn't know why!

III

August, 1995

Dear Mother,
Things are going well, but there's something bothering me. I lent some money to Jock. He got into a bit of a mess financially earlier this year, but he's not even tried to repay me. Yet it was a matter of life and death — his, that is. I remember him crying in my arms like a baby. Well, I found out one thing all right. Never lend money. Give it away freely if you can afford to, but don't ask for it back because you put that person in bondage to you. Do you see what I mean? You free a person from one set of chains and put them in *your* chains. So I helped him just when he needed it most and yet I made him a slave.

It was only a small amount of money, nevertheless you had written down on a piece of paper, "To be kept only for an emergency". But this *was* an emergency. He'd gotten into so much debt no wonder he was always looking fed up, saying he didn't know why. Until one day he told me the truth. There was a warrant for his arrest. I remember it vividly. Withdrawing my last few pounds out of my bank account for his bail. That night he stayed over. He felt 'protected under my wings', he said. We added up just how much he owed. The next day I withdrew your last penny, Mother, and took him the notes. Gave them to him and burst into floods of tears. I was in a state — going against your wishes and yet once a medium had told me that 'you love him as if you were his mother'.

'Now pay off everything!' I said to him.

Jock said he would pay me back. He never did. For months I would get up in the small hours of the night and shake my fist in the air with anger, especially when there were times when I could barely afford to eat. Then there were the times when he promised to be there if I ever needed him. And wasn't. I recall one Friday evening, not long after you passed over. Do you remember? It was cold. Icy cold. I felt your absence in my life terribly and I felt so alone. I phoned him, but he said, 'I'm not much good for you right now. I've had a busy day and I feel all stressed out, so I'm staying in. Sorry.'

I got into the car and drove. Miles and miles, not knowing where. Bereavement affects people like this. Finally I thought, 'How selfish of me. Poor Jock! I know what I'll do. I'll knock on his door with a can of lager and not stay, but that way I'm turning the negative into positive and helping someone else. All I'm doing now is feeling sorry for myself, not for Jock who's had a busy day.'

So I bought a couple of cans of lager and drove to his house. Where's his car, then? He was out. I sat and waited. He must have popped out for something. Time passed. And passed. And passed. I thought he was tired! He's gone for a night on the town. He must have. Yet maybe I'm wrong — but something tells me I'm right.

I drove home and phoned him. Not in. Midnight. 12:30. 1 a.m. 2 a.m. 3 .... 3:30 ....

So here we have it. Someone who I thought cared. And after me giving him your money, Mother .... Oh, God! What have I done?

The following morning I phoned again. Still not there. I drove to his house. The cans of lager were still on the doorstep.

My letter goes into his letterbox. As I feel it drop from my fingers, I wonder if I've jumped to conclusions. It read something like this:

Jock, I've always been there for you and just when I need you more than anytime in my life, you can't be there for me. You said you were tired and stressed out. Very f——g funny! I think it's time we went our separate ways for a while. Yet I'll always be here if you need me. I'm going away for a while. Don't know where. Got no money. I'll sleep in the car if I have to. Sorry our friendship is one-sided.

I got back home. Started throwing a few things into a suitcase. Phone rang. I knew it would be Jock. It was.

'Please come over.'

'I'm going away somewhere.'

'*Please* come over!'

I went over. I took one look at him as I entered the house. I could see he was sorry. His eyes said it. He was holding my letter.

'My aunt came up from Eastbourne. I stayed over with her at Dad's. We had a lot to get through, we haven't talked so much in ages.'

My heart sank. Poor Jock, thinking it was all his fault! That's what assuming does. Makes an ass out of me (ass-u-me). I was the selfish one.

'I'm sorry I wasn't there. I'll make it up to you,' he said. We had a hug and I left, feeling very guilty indeed.

But, Mother, there's a twist in the tale, isn't there?

If only Jock had known that two days later I was to bump into his aunt.

'Oh, what a shame,' she said. 'I was so looking forward to seeing my nephew, but he was going out for the night.'

'Which night?' I asked.

'Friday.'

My heart sank right to the bottom of my shoes. So I was right the first time. He had gone out for a night with the lads, just when I needed him most. Yet the worst part about it was that he had lied to me. I've decided to keep it to myself for now. When the time is right, I'll tell him.

I gave Jock my father's only possession — his ruby ring — as a token of our friendship. I wonder if he's still got it or pawned it?

I've told him to keep the money if it will "free him from bondage", but he says he wants to pay it back or he won't be happy. In which case I'll have to give him more time, but it makes me angry. I'll have to let these feelings go as quickly as possible if I'm going to be able to help other people.

Still, this just goes to prove that whatever life throws at you it's the learning experience that helps you become even stronger and able to understand others who have gone through the same experiences as yourself.

IV

August 16th, 1995

Dear Mother,
Something had been telling me not to go out. The "shadow of death feeling". But went against the warning, didn't I?

As I got out of the car to go to the newsagents I saw two girls and two guys watching me. As I walk back to the car they turn to face me. One of the guys (about twenty years old) shouts something. I get into the car, have to slow down behind a taxi to turn right. I look in my wing mirror. One of the guys is racing towards my car. I panic. *Oh, God!* .... I try to lock the car door from the inside .... the door is wrenched open ....

I'm dragged down by the hair and kicked and booted around the head over and over .... must've been sixteen times. He's swearing and I can't tell what he's shouting. I'm screaming .... It's a busy afternoon and not a single car stops. I see a red car drive past and its passengers just look on. The taxi at a standstill in front of me has people in the back who just stare. Nobody — absolutely *nobody* comes to my rescue.

Then it's all over. All four of them walk away. Slowly. As if nothing has happened. My ears are ringing. I'm in terrible pain. Blood is pouring from my head, my ears, my neck. My face aches and is already swollen. I'm in a state of shock. I don't know where I am or even who I am. The taxi driver gets out of his black cab and comes over to me.

'You've put me out of business,' he says.

'*What?*'

'You've gone into the back of me.'

I get out of the car and the nightmare continues. (During the attack I had been unable to put the car out of gear. Who could?)

'Look at the back of my cab!'

I can see absolutely nothing. If I've damaged his cab, I'll eat my hat. There's not a dent, a scratch — nothing! I must have just touched the back of his bumper with mine. That's all.

'Give us fifty quid,' he demands

'What?' I'm as dazed as can be.

'Give us fifty quid and we'll forget the whole thing and not bother with insurances.'

'Don't you realise I've been attacked and beaten up?'

'Didn't see a thing.'

(Strange. The passengers in the taxi witnessed the whole incident.)

'Fifty quid,' he insists.

Two men come over and run to get the police. The police didn't turn up. (I later found out that no one had phoned them.)

I'm shaking from shock. 'I've just been beaten up .... can't think straight .... why didn't you help me ....'

'Fifty quid!'

There are those things we ought not to have done .... Still in a state of shock we drive to my place. I give him fifty pounds. He hands me a receipt and leaves. I cry on the phone to Gabriela; later to Brian and Susan.

'I'm waiting for the police .... They're here now.'

The thugs were never found. That's one thing that isn't so glamorous about being recognised in the street. Nevertheless, a few nights later the same thing happened to a young lady in the same area.

She was not so lucky.

Brian and Gabriela came to see me the next day as if by magic, God bless them. What true friends! At the time I looked a sight, but it was truly a miracle that within a week you'd never have known what I had been through.

Karmic law says: What goes round, comes round.

It is already planned by a higher power what will happen to the thugs who attacked me. If not in this life, then in the next one. It is not for us to take the law into our own hands, however badly we have been made to suffer. I was certainly learning a thing or two. Like: 1) always lock your car when you get in it and 2) don't expect anyone to help you. If someone does at a time like that, then make them your friend for life!

Yet only a few months later I was able to find out why that experience did happen.

A wonderful gentleman came to see me. He was going to a psychiatrist because he couldn't cope with what had happened to him. He had been attacked in the same way, but at his family business and all his week's takings were stolen. The result was tranquillisers because he couldn't get over the shock.

It was then that I realised exactly what he was going through. I knew exactly what to say to him. I thanked God that I'd had the experience so I could help someone who had gone through the same thing. It was meant to be.

(But please, God — don't let it happen again!)

I must say a big thank you to my neighbour Janet for tending my wounds that terrible night and to Brian, Susan, Gabriela and Rustie for the support, prayers and strength they all gave me to get over it.

IV

August, 1995

Dear Mother,

I do hope that people reading this book will not assume that I am trying to sound like the great I AM. Every learning experience I have had since your passing has been meant so that I can sympathise and help many people. I truly am ready to work with and for Spirit in a big way as their servant, messenger and guide.

I know I have a lot of work to do!

Chapter Eight

September, 1995

Dear Mother,

Met someone wonderful, Mother. Love at first sight. Don't know how this person feels about me. I've given out a lot of energy lately, trying to build up his confidence. I know you understand how I feel. My spiritual work is not just work but a way of life; I need someone who loves me for myself and not for what they can get. O.k., I'm psychic, but very often those who touch our hearts you can't always "see through" them right away. Until it's too late. I spend a lot of time giving out love and it's a nice thought that maybe one person can give love to me without expecting anything in return. Shall I say something of the way I feel or not? Turned over a few tarot cards. Outcome: heartbreak!

The Moon and Stars do guide me
along my Spiritual pathway,
I am loved by many — but not by one
so I am alone.
I try not to block out the Sun
with tears of ingratitude for life. But ....

The arms I need to enfold me are not there.
They are the arms of my imagination only.

And yet I dream.

Putting others onto their chosen pathway,
only to find that I myself have lost my way.

Ever seeking — ever searching.
I hear angel voices and yet they are the voices
of lost souls.

I reach out to them and know that they hear
my call. So I can send them into the Light.

If no one should ever love me I shall not
have failed if each day I can help someone
to grow in love spiritually. To forgive themselves,
to not judge themselves. To love themselves.

I cannot speak the words of love I wish to
utter — for fear of rejection.

And yet I may be wrong ....

No, Mother. I wasn't wrong. I did speak the words. My intuition was right. That person was out to use me only and then was gone. Yet again another learning experience so that if the next person who came to me had had the same problem I would know what to say. To listen and to understand.

One of the problems in the world today: people won't listen!

II

October, 1995

Dear Mother,
There's a poem in the form of a plaque in Brian and Susan's home. Beneficial to everyone, I feel.

Happiness is like a Butterfly,
The more you chase it, the more it will elude you.
But when you turn your attention to other things,
Then it comes and rests softly on your shoulder.

(anon.)

Plus another useful saying:
CHANGE WHAT YOU CAN AND DON'T WORRY ABOUT THE REST.

III

October, 1995

Dear Mother,
Been photographed and interviewed by the Telegraph magazine, full colour feature will be out in December. Claire, who interviewed me, wanted to know about 'proof of psychic energy'. I said to her like I say to everybody, 'I don't prove anything to anyone. When it's time they get their answers.'

She wanted to tape record the interview as well as write it. I told her:

'When tape recorders and electrical equipment come near me, they usually break down or go wrong.'

(This is something to do with the energy levels we give off. It happens to lots of psychics, not just to me!)

'Oh, no, it won't go wrong,' said Claire. 'Mine's a very expensive piece of equipment.'

O.k. Recording equipment is switched on. Claire speaks. Fine! I speak. Nothing!

She tries again.

'It won't work when you speak,' she says.

I go out into the hall.

'O.k.,' she calls. 'It's working perfectly now!'

I enter the room. Click! *Nothing!*

One has to smile

'I told you you'd get proof if it was meant to be, without my trying to prove anything to you!'

After Claire left, I felt uneasy and thought, 'I don't know why. She's been with me over four hours, but I wish she was back. I feel something's wrong ....'

An hour later Steve and I were driving along the motorway to the first night of the Royal Ballet's "Carmina Burana". He switched on the car radio for the news.

'A serious accident happened an hour ago. The commuter train to Birmingham has come off the rails. No serious injuries.'

'Oh, God!'

'You don't do anything by halves, do you?' said Steve.

Well, of course it had nothing to do with me, but it was certainly a bizarre feeling.

I phoned Claire the following day, expecting (assuming again!) her to say, 'Oh, very psychic — you didn't predict *that*!' but instead she said,

'You really are psychic, aren't you? My tape recorder's working perfectly now!'

I personally believe we all have this same energy that we transform into healing energy. The word "spiritual" in the dictionary actually means, "living". So when asking Spirit for help we are asking the "living", as there is no death.

I also say to so many people:

I — and all true mediums (though there are a few) do *not* contact the so-called "dead". They contact *us*, the medium. It is *their* choice, should they wish to communicate in some way or another. Not ours! We mediums are just the catalyst, as I said earlier. A person in Spirit will choose a medium to "come through" for a particular sitter.

PSYCHIC PROTECTION

You know, Mother, I never thought I would need psychic protection. Opening up and closing down. Yet I have found out that it is very important indeed. There are without doubt good and evil forces in Spirit and when you open yourself up to Spirit you can open yourself up to all manner of things. Therefore I have written some useful ideas. Thanks to Brian for a few of the tips given and for his help to me in these matters.

(It's like when people consult a ouija board. Just to sit there and say, 'Is there anybody there?' is asking for trouble! Of course there's somebody there — good and bad!)

When meditating or doing any psychic work or when retiring for the night:

1. Imagine that you walk outside your front door and walk around your property — across the neighbours' gardens if you have them — and back in through your front door. With each step you take, you leave behind a wall of fire of protection all around your property. Imagine and believe that *nothing* evil from this world or the next can break through this impenetrable barrier, the wall of fire of protection.
   Within this circle of protection you are only keeping in love and light and only Spirit of Good are allowed to be with you within your circle of fire. No other force or entity is permitted.

2. Light a candle: preferably a pure white one as an offering — a gift of love to Spirits of good and of love. A token of your thanks to them for the good you are willing to do for others that they are helping you to do.

3. Pray. Thank God and Spirit for helping you, protecting you and keeping you safe. Thank God for all your experiences and the love given from him that you can give to others.

4. Rainbows of light and love. Imagine when you are to sit in meditation or lie down to go to sleep that a beautiful rainbow of translucent colours rises from the left side of you, surrounds you completely and falls to the right hand side of you. Then imagine each colour drifts down to the top of your head — starting with red and sinks down to each chakra point. (See diagram.) Let it rest there for a few seconds and then allow each colour to drift down through the rest of your body and finally out through the soles of the feet, taking away all negativity that you may have within you and replacing it with health, light, love, inner strength and universal energy. These will remain with you. Remember that you have encased yourself in a rainbow of protective light and love and that nothing can harm you. Imagine each colour healing any part of your body or any part of your mind.

5. Protect yourself by using geranium or lavender oil. Either burn some in an essential oil burner or a few drops on a lamp ring (placed over a light bulb) and a few drops on the backs of your hands and on the wrists. Geranium is a

powerful cleanser of the aura and when doing healing work will actually prevent you from transferring the feelings of the illness of the person you are trying to help. Lavender is cleansing and healing. For most of my spiritual healing work I use the colours purple and violet. These colours are the most beneficial for spiritual healing. They are the most calming and relaxing, but at the same time the strongest and most powerful healing shades.

The Chakras

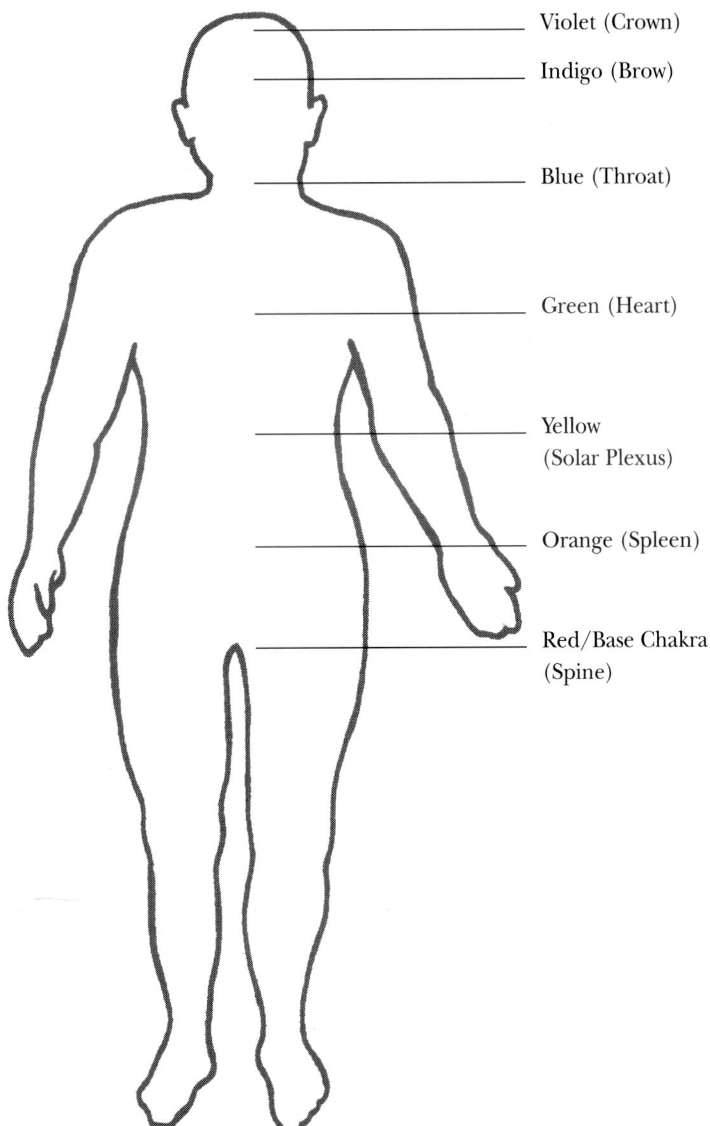

It is also an advantage that the healing of certain ailments associated with parts of the body can be helped dramatically with the use of certain music and sounds in the "key of". For example: headaches can be alleviated if you listen to music in the key of A. Examples are: piano concertos, symphonies, etc.

1. Base chakra (red): middle C. Good for colds and flu. Especially for back-ache.
2. Spleen (orange): D. Reproductive system and emotional balance. Rids anger.
3. Solar plexus (yellow): E. Constipation, sickness, migraine associated with upset stomachs.
4. Heart (green): F. Lungs, circulation, heart disorders. **Not cancer**. Cancer sufferers must never wear green. Green is a strengthener and being the colour of nature, it makes things grow.
5. Throat (blue): G. Asthma, lungs, throat, fevers, colds.
6. Brow (indigo): B. Nervous system and stress, insomnia, problems with bones.
7. Crown (violet): A. Headaches, strengthening the mind, body and spirit. Helps to remove blockages that stand between the spiritual and the physical. Helps to maintain good grounding in all spiritual work.

So these are just a few ideas for people to use, Mother. Let's hope readers will try some of these methods, as they really do work. Yes, yes, o.k. I know you're by my side now and you want me to talk a little more about doing Spiritual healing ....

It is important, when doing healing work, to remember that

a. you don't have to try too hard, but allow universal energy and Spirit — still all from God — to come through you.
b. don't — as I have learned myself — use up all your own energy. Ask Spirit for help. They will give you all the energy and healing you need. There is no need to drain yourself.

Imagine, after lighting a candle for Spirit, burning the necessary oils and saying a prayer to thank Spirit for their help, that when you lay your hands upon someone or even resting on their auric field you are withdrawing the pain; when you feel that the time is just right, replace what you have "taken out" with healing, strength, universal energy, love and light. If you see any lights or shadows, concentrate there. Spirit do guide healers to the "spot". Remember, Spirit will give you all the energy and healing you need. Usually a person you are healing will feel very relaxed and may go to sleep. This is good, as they are obviously trusting in you, the healer. Also, it is a sign from Spirit. They are helping that person to relax so that you can do your work for them.

Always imagine, like I do, that your hands have become like a sponge soaking up all negativity and replacing it with positivity. You will know when to stop your session of healing. Afterwards the so-called patient will feel very calm and relaxed — without a care in the world. You should feel calm, yet physically and mentally strong as though you could do it all over again. This is good. But if you feel “all in” and really drained, then something is wrong. Usually because you’ve been giving out your energy.

When healing, just believe in the power of Spirit and of God, and believe in yourself as the catalyst between Spirit and patient.

Afterwards, shower, change your clothing, shake and brush your clothing, and wash your hands so that you are getting rid of all negative vibrations. Yet don’t make it obvious to the person you’ve been healing. You certainly don’t want them to feel bad about coming to see you!

Chapter Nine

October, 1995

Dear Mother,

Well, what about a bit of positive thinking to start the day? What about waking up in the morning, throwing off the duvet and shouting 'WOW! Isn't life exciting?' Go down the garden path and yell out, 'YES!' Believe in yourself. Forgive yourself. Move forward each day with the knowledge that yesterday was o.k. and today can be even better. What a great day, *every day*, to make positive affirmations with sheer joy and love of life, whatever our circumstances and however rich, poor, famous or otherwise we may be.

What can you say? How about:

'I am a special person and in tune with myself.'

'Each day, in every way, I'm going to be confident and in control.'

'Each day I'm going to do something special — if it isn't for me, then I'll do it for someone else.'

Go and hug someone at least five times a day.

Remember: each day you wake up feeling depressed, go look at yourself in the bathroom mirror and growl and roar just like a lion, growl until you've growled all the tensions away and you find you've burst out laughing!

We have to remember that it's not wrong to feel "down" sometimes. It's only natural. If we were on a high all the time, we wouldn't get the balance right.

Let's not forget about bringing universal energy down to us: reach out your arms and grasp it with your hands. Bring it down into your heart and your mind. Keep it within you so that you can use it for the benefit for others. You can always keep some energy within yourself too.

The world is full of energy and it's given to us from God. Let's not waste it!

The gemstone hematite is an excellent stone to give you energy. You can buy it as a ring to wear. I find that I have to remember to remove my hematite ring at bedtime or I'd have so much energy that I wouldn't get to sleep at all!

Clear quartz for clarity of mind — clear thinking. Rose quartz helps you to love others as well as to love yourself. It also helps you to forgive.

I bless stones like rose quartz all the time for lovers. It's so romantic for someone to purchase two small pieces of rose quartz for me to bless them and energize them.

Then for that person to give one of them to their friend or lover as a token of love and affection.

It's easy to meditate holding a piece of clear quartz and rose quartz in each hand. Forget you're holding them as you just allow your mind to relax, breathe deeply and allow yourself to drift into meditation and relaxation as much as is possible at the time. You will find after this period of meditation that you feel calmer, more relaxed, confident, with love of yourself and others and with clarity of mind. Remember, after periods of meditation your powers of predicting will come to the fore. Never try too hard, just allow anything to come gently into your mind and then jot it down on paper.

Pendulum power is another spiritual tool which can be extremely beneficial. I use a phantom quartz, so named because it has another quartz growing inside it. The genie of the magic lamp is where the true meaning of a phantom quartz originates. Pendulums can be used to give "yes" and "no" answers and there are plenty of books available today to help guide you on how to use a pendulum properly, known as "dowsing". You can even ask your pendulum if you are on the right road by dowsing over a road map. If you've taken the wrong road your pendulum will naturally swing to the left (or in an anti-clockwise direction). Then ask the pendulum to stop spinning. Command it to stop. It will. Then ask it to direct you onto the road that you should be taking. It will!

I use my pendulum nowadays mainly to give people energy and also for healing. Your pendulum will let the healer (you) know if there is a certain part of a person's body that needs healing by simply holding the pendulum over parts of a person's body.

For example, if someone has a broken arm I just take their arm in my left hand, hold the pendulum in my right hand and hold it over the arm. I say a prayer and ask Spirit to help me to help, to heal and to also give that person energy. Once the pendulum has built up its own divine universal energy I ask that person to take the energy into themselves, into the part of the body that needs to be healed — in this instance a broken arm. Then allow the disease and pain to go down to the soles of their feet and right into the ground where the negative energy can be transformed into positive energy again, so that no energy is wasted but can always be turned into good use.

I remember one day at Brian's house my pendulum was spinning around, all the more as I was thinking of energy when suddenly .... Buzzzz!

The music I had been playing went off, the electric clocks all flashed on to zero — even the video!

All I could think of was, 'Wait until they get home!' The tape-recorders, CDs, lights, phones that have gone wrong after a visit to Brian's house is nobody's business. Like one winter's night after I'd gone back to my place and the phone rang.

'Thank you!' said Brian. 'Since you left, my outside lights won't go off!'

One day I was in my front room and on a real high of energy. I had my stereo on and was writing. I dropped my pen, bent over to pick it up — and the volume went right down! I stood up — the volume went up again!

Incredible!

I was there all evening, standing up and bending over. Great! Tried it while sitting down, facing the stereo. Put my arm up into the air and brought it down again. Super! Don't need to get up to turn it down. Then I got annoyed! I only had to move or cross my legs and the volume would go up, down. At one stage the whole system went off! And they say that there's no such thing as energy! All the same .... If you can affect electrical equipment like that, then it's that same energy that we have to give out for healing!

Makes sense, doesn't it, Mother?

A day of "going for Life with a capital L" can be pretty exhausting, so don't forget to calm down at bedtime and do some deep breathing exercises when you get into bed. Breathe in through the nose, counting 3. Hold the breath counting 3 and breath out through the mouth counting 3. Breathing in positivity, breathing out negativity. Start at 200. So it's 200 — breathe in — hold — breathe out and so on. 199, 198 .... If you lose count start again at 200, but I can assure you that when you get to about 194 you'll be asleep!

What a positive chapter that was! WOW!

II

October, 1995

Dear Mother,

Remember Jock, Mother? The one I lent the money to? He's lent some money to a close friend and they've gone abroad for a few weeks! Money he should be paying back to me! He keeps promising, but he's never even tried to repay me. And yet he can lend someone nearly £400 — it doesn't seem fair. I don't believe I will ever get it back now. How could he have used me like this? Yet there's this bond between us I can't break. Told me he's gonna sell his car and pay me back then. I've still got to believe he will ....

Really had to reassure someone today who told me there had been no contact from a deceased relative who had always said they would "come back". This is because of the Spirit needing to rest. This is why so many people get disappointed when no contact is made. After a suffering period on this earth plane — for example, from cancer — the Spirit has also suffered as well as the physical body. It takes time, so we have to be patient. Someone in Spirit may choose not to visit any of us. After all, they are now on a different plane and have to live a new life. Also with things such as fatal car accidents, it has been a "shock" to the Spirit. Again, that Spirit has to rest. When the time is right and Spirit is ready they will contact us if they choose to. We all have to remember this.

III

November, 1995

Dear Mother,
It's twelve months today since you passed over. The leaves didn't look or fall as beautifully as last year. I can't believe this year has gone by so quickly. I should be celebrating the fact that you are in the world of Spirit and are with Dad and Granma now. Yet somehow I'm finding it difficult to take it all in. There's been some good times and bad times since you've been gone. I wondered if you would be back to visit me today of all days. But, no. Obviously you haven't needed to.

I went with Gabriela to Beatties department store in Wolverhampton just like you and I always used to and had the same meal: salmon and cucumber sandwiches, and Earl Grey tea. Gabriela commented that she felt you were with us all the while. I just felt sad. But it was wonderful to spend the time with Gabriela. She was wearing your best emerald green jacket that I bought for you, so it was as if you were with us. Remember the day I gave it to her, Mother? Gabriela looked fabulous in it, as if it was made for her, and tears filled my eyes when she appeared by the lounge doorway of her home when she first put it on. That's one thing I'll never regret. We can hang on to possessions of a deceased relative, but we have to "let go" eventually, although it breaks your heart at the time. Someone in Spirit has no need of their old earthly belongings. We have to create our future lives for us. Naturally it's up to the individual to choose the best time to sort out their deceased's belongings. There's no rush and eventually you yourself know when the time is right.

Letting go are two words that I have a feeling I'll be using a lot from now on. They're probably two of the hardest words to put into practice. We can't move forward unless we "let go".

The commemoration of someone's passing is always a difficult time. We cannot erase from our minds what really did happen. Once those first twelve months are over you find that you have become stronger with the knowledge that your loved ones have been called to Spirit at their chosen time. We will indeed be united with them again when, and only when, we are called at our allotted time. If we grieve far too long that person in Spirit will not be happy in the Spirit world and, after all, we don't want that for them, do we? Remember as well that when a relative or friend who has passed over appears to you in your dreams, they are nearly always looking wonderful — more wonderful than they ever used to look. That is how they are now in the Spirit world. Remember that if you have ever lost a baby or a young child that person who you would have guided and protected now becomes your Guardian Angel. They continue to grow up, not only in the Spirit world but often alongside you. They grow in the Spirit halls of learning. No matter how terrible the feelings of loss you might have, you have to satisfy your hearts and your minds that they have been called to Spirit to live and work in that dimension for a reason.

No one dies. There is no death.

I recall meeting a gentleman in a petrol station, of all places. His son in Spirit, now about eleven years of age, was standing right next to him. I *had* to tell him. It meant a lot to him to finally know that his son was o.k. Also, it is important to remember that we are all born with a Spirit Guide. Our guide is chosen for us before our birth. All of us are protected by Spirit and as long as we stick to the straight and narrow our guides will help us. If we fall off that very narrow line and commit crimes of theft, rape, murder, etc., our guides will not only leave us, but will leave us for good unless we amend the error of our ways.

No, Mother. I never thought I'd give your emerald jacket away, but I knew you wished Gabriela to have it. On the way home I looked in the rear-view mirror. Just for an instant I saw your face and felt your presence. You came out in the car to be with us that evening. God bless you and keep you safe.

IV

November, 1995

Dear Mother,

I've met so many wonderful people, Mother. Plus a lot of very sad ones, but all of them I've meant to meet to help them find their way. Done quite a few talks to different groups and societies. Gone down well each time. Talks about confidence and how to develop your underlying psychic abilities. Made quite a few radio appearances too. Enjoyed every minute of them. Can't think how or why they've not banned me from the air! What with the size of my crystal balls jokes .... Yet people listening in have really responded to me. Will be making my first appearance on BBC Radio Shropshire this month. Looking forward to it. I feel really drawn to Shropshire, as though somehow my roots are there. Becoming a happy medium, I suppose it's only right that I should be on medium wave!

Had a fascinating experience after doing an after-dinner talk at Bewdley. Saw flying saucer lights circling me, going round and round, coloured and white lights. At first I nearly crashed the car. (This was to happen again — twice in fact — in the same place over Cannock Chase and between 12.30 a.m. — 1 a.m.!) A local newspaper quoted me as saying, 'If it happens again I'll stop the car, get out and if I'm taken away to Jupiter or wherever, then I'll be happy to go.'

V

December, 1995

Dear Mother,

That's it! I've found heaven here on earth in the form of what must be a psychic's dream shop.

'Don't spend any money until we get to Solstice,' said Sue over and over as she,

Brian and myself did a tour of Shropshire's spiritual gift shops. Of course .... I ignored the voice of one who knew better and thought each shop was great until we reached Solstice. Brian loves to tell the story of my first visit there. I could smell the incense from outside and could hear the music drifting through and giving a sparkle to the chilly, frost air. And then I made my first entrance .... and fell down the steps .... my hair got caught on the windchimes .... Clang! Clang! I seemed to throw myself right into the shop and into the CD display stand. What better place to literally spend money you haven't really got? Every type of music is there for healing, for energy, for meditation — about eight hundred kinds. Oils, incense, books, every type of gemstone, clothing, Egyptian statues, Chinese statues, Indian statues, throws, rugs, embroidered clothing — and the jewellery!

Eventually Brian's voice piped up: 'Are we going or have we got to drag him out by the hair?'

So .... I've been back ever since, on every occasion and at every spare moment and it's not just the shop, it's the people!

More about them all later, but I must tell you about one visit in particular. Bridget, the owner, was with her mother and her mother really took to me. (Probably because I knocked a whole box of crystals off a shelf and was on my hands and knees with Ray, Bridget's husband, picking them all up. You know — one of those awful occasions when you wish the ground would just open up and swallow you!) I came into the shop to look for some incense called Cleopatra and was told about the following conversation:

Bridget: 'He's looking for Cleopatra.'

Bridget's mother: 'Will I do instead?' (!)

If there's anything you need, Solstice is the place. Whether it's a crystal ball, a set of tarot cards or just a birthday card, it's there. In fact, they will send anything anywhere in the world if you know exactly what you want.

VI

December 15th, 1996

Dear Mother,
What a strange way to celebrate your birthday! Going as a celebrity at the opening of a new nightclub in Birmingham. There are stars of stage and screen there. A few members from the cast of "Eastenders" and many Shakespearean actors. And I'm here with them! Only last year I wanted to die because of the loss of you. You *must* be waving a magic wand in heaven.

Yet I have to admit it. I'm too spiritually minded for any type of nightclub. I have to be with other spiritually minded people to find happiness. It's become a way of life now. I wonder if you approve of me going to the nightclub? Anyhow, it was certainly a taste of the high life you usually only read about.

VII

December 23rd, 1995

Dear Mother,

Just completed a two-hour phone-in again on BBC Radio Shropshire on the Colin Young show. I've given out some of the biggest messages ever in my life to give hope to people. It even has baffled me how I knew when different people phoned in that their mothers, husbands, grandparents, etc. were in Spirit, but I did and the messages given from Spirit to those people I *know* will have made their Christmas.

Got back really late after visiting Brian and Sue. My answering machine was pulsating and flashing on and off because it was full of messages. Most of them like, 'My name is Elsie. Please phone me back and tell me my future. Thank you.'

That's one lesson I've learned. Don't phone back.

'Would you like to make an appointment for a sitting?'

'I don't have to pay, do I? I thought you could just tell me.'

'Well, I am self-employed.'

'Do I have to pay .... With money?'

'Well, it is my time and I still have my bills to pay ....'

But one lady was meant to meet me. Beautiful Brenda Whincup — and you will read more about her later!

VIII

Christmas, 1995

Dear Mother,

Still lost without you! You know, I've not felt you near me at all lately. I guess Christmas in Heaven must be better! Santa came in the form of Gabriela and John, Steve, Brian and Susan. Then caught the flu. Drat! I was looking forward to meeting Brenda.

I'm lying in bed. Answering machine's on. It's mid-afternoon and I'm right in the middle of the flu and feel terrible. The phone rings. I hear Rustie's voice come over.

'Mystic Ed....ward! It's Rustie! Are you there? Well, I'll keep chatting in case you're there .... How about coming on the show on New Year's Eve? It's a celebrity phone-in and we can have fun ....'

By this time I've managed to drag myself down the hall, flannelette pyjamas, Mother's bedsocks, "Teddy Bear" hot water bottle and all!

'Hello, Wustie. I've an awful cowd. Can't bweathe.'

'Well, you'll be feeling better I'm sure by Sunday and if you're not we'll just do it down the line.'

'It'll be a miwacle, Wustie.'

And it was a miracle!

Only three days later Gabriela, also invited to be on the show, and I are there at Pebble Mill.

Two hours later I had spoken to and done tarot readings live on air for Diana Moran (the Green Goddess) Victor Spinnetti (actor), Tessa Sanderson (athlete), Russell Grant (astrologer), Madeline Bell (singer), Paul from a pop group called "Juice" and wonderful Ruth Madoc (from Hi de Hi), who said my words were in 'the language of heaven'.

What an experience! I recall the first time on Rustie's show when I did a live prediction for "Slade" singer Noddy Holder.

Well — I've become the Psychic to the Stars all right!

I even gave twelve months astrological predictions on air and fell apart laughing. I think when I got to Taurus that "bountiful bulls" sounded like something else!

What a way to end 1995, Mother! Boy, have you been around! Something's building me up for something. Makes me feel I'll have my own show one day at this rate.

Wherever you are — Happy New Year, Mother, and thank you for your guidance.

I wonder what 1996 will hold. I dare say something else exciting. Probably some sad times. Something's telling me that I may even find users, takers, and that maybe I may get my heart broken yet again. But I'm ready. I'm happy and I've got some lovely friends, Mother. No use giving up now, I've come too far. The main things is that I've got my name known so that I can reach out to so many people. To heal, to guide, to regress. That is what my ambition is at this moment: to help people to find their way. I'll continue to be "Happy Medium" Mystic Ed and that definitely appeals to the public. When they meet me for sittings they will know how much Spirit can help them.

(Addition to the end of New Year's Eve, 1995)

Because of my sudden popularity I had people love me for what and who I am and what I am trying to achieve. But the sad part is that you then get hated and feared and envied by close friends (none of those mentioned, I hasten to add!) who you've known a long time. Also, sadly, by other mediums because of where you've got and they haven't. One medium tried to make me "crumble to dust", but it didn't work. Mediums should be glad when they hear of another medium's success. After all, we should all be working together in our own ways destined for us and therefore should rejoice in each other's ways of shining a golden light in the paths of many who are living in darkness. Often criticism has made me stronger and more determined to push on and I know Spirit is even more on my side. I've also got used to newspapers misquoting me. Apparently I was quoted as saying that the 'Queen Mother will be dogged by health problems' .... *I never said that!*

I shall never forget a medium taking me by the hand and saying, 'Without your celebrity side you'd be nothing!'

Is that a way to spread love to others or not?

Chapter Ten

January – March, 1996

Dear Mother,

A new year has begun and a new era. Met wonderful poet Brenda Whincup. Everything predicted for her came true before she even left the house, like: I told her she would have a new car, burgundy in colour. Her husband came in, saying that he had seen a new car — and it was burgundy in colour! I feel I've known Brenda all my life and her mother in Spirit is always present when we are together. I've predicted a book-signing for her, too. (In fact, this has happened — November 1996!) Who would have thought that this lady would one day be a guest on my own radio show? It was through her that I met Diana Mills of Blue Dragon Press, publisher of this book. The whole purpose of Blue Dragon is to give hope, inspiration and love to people of all nationalities and ages, whether rich or poor, and the "right" people seem to have come into Diana's life as authors. (It won't be long before she makes a public appearance on our screens and also on American TV ....)

To go back to the lady who said that without my celebrity side I'd be nothing .... well, I saved a gentleman's life today. In his relationships he'd been used so much that he'd had enough and was going to end his life. I asked God and Spirit for protection and guidance as he and I talked well into the night over the telephone. Somehow, thanks to God, he didn't commit suicide and now has a happy life with someone who loves him totally. Thank God I was on the other end of the phone that night! If I had been out it would have been too late. That is what life is all about — shining light into the darkness.

I've been told by Spirit that I have several duties to perform, Mother. One is to send earth-bound Spirits into the Light. A friend visited me not long ago and left behind her the smell of ether. This awful fragrance was associated with the passing over of her husband. For a week the smell remained. The poor gentleman had stayed behind spiritually and wouldn't go on to his new spiritual home. I did what I had to do and sent him on his way into the Light. The smell of ether went. This is something that I do a lot of now. Many poor souls remain earthbound because they are hanging on too tightly to their homes or families and need to be reassured that they have now played their part on this earth plane. So that they can go to the next world and find peace.

Another duty, told to me by Spirit, is to take the burdens away from other people.

To take away all the emotions they are hanging on to, so that they can move on with their lives. My duty is to then transport this negativity that they have passed on to me and send it back into the universe. In this way it can be turned into positive energy so that nothing has been wasted. I can assure anyone reading this that it is nothing for them to worry about when they throw their burdens at me. I do not take the symptoms on myself. I just ask people to give away to me what is holding them back.

Many, many people I have met have done the same as I! They have learnt the true value of life and how important it is.

TRANSFIGURATION

Many mediums "transfigurate", i.e. the Spirit communicating with the medium comes through. Often the voice and features change. Occasionally this has happened with me. I was only really aware of this when someone told me that my face had changed when talking about someone's deceased father-in-law. Now it happens at lot. Some mediums do put on quite an act, throwing back their heads, shaking all over and yelling out, 'Ooh! Oooh! The Vibrationsss .... I can feel my GUIDE COMING THROUGH!'

Wow! What a performance. Not to be taken seriously, I hasten to add.

When a guide comes through it is a feeling of complete calm and control. A feeling of peace, love and yet a powerful feeling all at the same time. It is important to remember when it happens to you that it is not spooky or frightening, but an experience of complete beauty. We have to remember to talk to our guides and to thank them for using us as a channel to help others. A friend of mine who is going to be a great medium has his guide come through regularly. It is then when his messages come through loud and clear, and my home is filled with a great inner peace and security. Our own personal guides are, as stated previously, with us through life to do just that: guide. So we must trust them totally.

THE OCCULT

I must stress clearly and simply: I do not dabble in any darker force, i.e. black magic. I believe that God has given us our gifts. The word occult simply means "what is hidden, unseen". Straightaway it conjures up thoughts of black magic, naked (or as used in spiritual terms, "skyclad") virgins placed on altars as sacrifices and satanic rituals. And yes, the occult does certainly have its fair share of people that do this, but these are very grave steps to take. If you play with fire, you are likely to get burned!

The study of occultism is basically the study of an ancient knowledge — that which is hidden — not immediately obvious to us. It all depends on how we use this knowledge that psychics study and which has been passed down to us over thousands of years. How we can contribute to our planet, the universe and everyone in it; how we can help make the world a better place filled with love. This is our contribution: using this divine knowledge for the benefit of others. So when you hear the word "occult", don't always be put off. If we didn't study all things — good and not so good — we wouldn't know the difference and this is why it is important that we obtain a basic knowledge of these things. Like is like that, isn't it? Good and bad. We have to study to obtain wisdom. So that we can teach others the right things and how to get on the right course of action in their own daily lives.

My belief in God is a strong belief. Through him all things are made and it is thanks to him for giving us all our gifts so that we can share our love with others. He gives us the power to do all things.

II

January, 1996

Dear Mother,

When you need energy — go hug a tree. Ask its permission first. Then thank it and throw your arms around it. Love it! Give it some energy and receive some in return! Tell the world!

I haven't felt your presence around lately, Mother. I want to so much, but obviously you are busy doing other things. Was meditating today, Sunday. Opened my eyes and a man's voice said loudly in Spirit, 'You're going on a thirty minute TV programme.'

'Am I?' I thought. 'Wonder what?'

III

Monday, January, 1996

Dear Mother,

'Are you ready to be filmed for TV?' asked an excited Gabriela over the telephone.

'Er .... well, yes .... I suppose so ....'

' "Can't Cook, Won't Cook" with Ainsley Harriot. It'll be on for thirty minutes and *you're* going to do the cooking!'

'Me? Cooking? Cooking what? Can't I just use a tin opener and bung it into the oven and pray?'

She laughed. I laughed. Us two together on TV! Is the world ready for us? I phoned her back a few minutes later, remembering the message from the voice yesterday saying, 'You're going on a thirty minute TV programme.'

'Gabriela, how long did you say it would be on air for?'

'Half an hour, Ed.'

Whatever next, Mother! I've made loads of radio appearances, now it's TV time. Photographers are wanting to probe me with their zoom lenses yet again!

DIANA DORS, MARILYN MONROE, MARLENE DIETRICH. PAUL KEMP, SANDRA FIELD AND ME

I am proud to possess a beautiful porcelain bust of Marilyn Monroe, Mother. I first saw her in an antique shop, of all places! I just had to have her. It was in November, the actual commemoration of your passing, Mother. I could barely afford to buy it at the time, but a voice kept saying to me, 'buy it, buy it' — and so I did. She is just like real. People who claim not to be psychic see auras around her. The first time that the bust "turned" was when a gifted medium called Pam was with me. She had been to see me for a private sitting and afterwards we sat together in the lounge, indulging in a cup of tea and a cigarette. Suddenly my gaze was fixed upon Marilyn. Across her face drifted beautifully coloured circular spirit lights in a way that cannot be described on paper. As I gazed in amazement I yelled out, 'She's moved!'

'Yes,' said Pam calmly — shaken, but not stirred. 'And she still is. She's turning.'

Before this Marilyn had been facing the TV set which was situated directly opposite in the corner of the lounge. Now, very very slowly, she had turned about three feet and was facing the door. For two whole hours we both witnessed it and sat calmly watching. It wasn't the bust of Marilyn that moved, but it was the "force behind the power", so to speak. What an incredible and amazing thing to happen! Two days later I told my dear friend Gabriela about this while we sat in the huge restaurant of the Nottingham-based TV centre, waiting to be filmed for BBC 1's "Can't Cook, Won't Cook" with Ainsley Harriot.

'Oh, I've gone all cold, Ed,' she said. 'You've not seen it, have you?'

'Seen what?'

'I think you'd better look up, Ed.'

I looked up. Suspended from the ceiling directly over our tables was a life-size stone statue of Marilyn Monroe!

The filming of the show was a huge success — my first "taste" of television. Though I hate to admit it, I wouldn't have fed my stuffed Polish cabbage to a starving pussy! To this day people still remember me for it. I even began to call myself the "Confused Clairvoyant Cabbage Stuffer of Cannock"!

Since then I have had many, many experiences with Marilyn. I have seen many beautiful auras around her time after time — and always at nine o'clock in the evening. I've also seen the spirit faces of Marlene Dietrich and a very young Bette Davis in place of Marilyn. All stars coming through to the Psychic to the Stars. When Miss Davis's face shone through, all I could hear was, 'Margaret. Margaret Merrill.' We have to remember to be patient and wait. Spirit reveal to us what they want us to know at their chosen time and not when we want it to be. This should be how a true medium should work. A true medium's work comes from the heart and *never* tries to "conjure up" Spirit. It is Spirit's choice to communicate with us.

One of the most fascinating and wonderful experiences with Marilyn came about one Friday evening. There I was scrubbing away in the kitchen — like you do — when a distant voice from Spirit whispered, 'Go into the front room.' So I did as told. The blinds in the lounge were open and the street lights outside shone directly onto Marilyn in the calm blackness of night.

'You will get your answer on Thursday,' I heard her whisper sweetly.

I stood there in the dark, my eyes transfixed on her — standing there with my Mr Muscle in one hand and a J-cloth in the other (whoops! advertising!) — and said aloud:

'What answer? I haven't asked a question yet!'

And that was it. I remember telling Brian about it over the telephone. 'Marilyn — talking to me. *Me!* Little me in the west midlands — Cannock, of all places. It's not exactly Hollywood, is it?'

'Why not you? She's in Spirit like everyone in Spirit. She can talk to who she chooses,' said Brian, who always knows the right answers, God love 'im!

I recalled how Tommy Cooper "came through" to the wonderful, late Doris Stokes when she was on stage in Stoke-on-Trent. (By the way, many mediums have seen Doris standing by my side in Spirit.)

'But what answer? *What* answer?' I kept repeating.

'Well,' said Brian, 'We'll wait and see what happens on Thursday.'

THE ANSWER CAME

On Thursday that following week I received a telephone call from BBC Pebble Mill TV Studios. I was requested to go on live television, BBC 1's "Good Morning with Anne and Nick", as a psychic expert.

So that was my answer to a question I hadn't even asked. God bless you, Marilyn!

And so I went on live TV. I took my bust of Marilyn with me. It was so funny. Brian came with me and carried Marilyn safely for me wrapped up in a large yellow bath towel so she wouldn't get damaged. So there we both appeared, Marilyn and myself on live TV together. Marilyn stood proudly on a pedestal next to the charming and very witty presenter Nick Owen. I went on the show along with two other psychics, Craig and Jane Hamilton-Parker, authors of *The Psychic's Workbook.*

I have a video of that live performance. Just at the point of discussing auras with me, Nick Owen asks, 'Have I got an aura, Mystic Ed?'

To which I reply, 'You've got a wonderful one — it's *enormous* Nick!'

(Chortle, chortle — the cameramen just fall about laughing.)

A beautiful aura of Marilyn literally floats across to Nick and when stopped, the film shows a stunningly beautiful "double image" of her.

Late that night I felt it only right to offer a toast to Marilyn:

'There, you're a star! Thirty years later and you're a star again, but this time in *Spirit* yet on live TV!'

I often wonder how many viewers saw this ....

The story continues:

In August 1995 I met Paul Kemp — a young, ambitious and very talented reporter/ journalist who came to see me to do a full page feature for the Cannock, Lichfield and Rugeley Mercury. If there is talent in a writer, it's certainly there with him. He wrote a wonderful feature entitled "Back Through the Mists of Time" and included a lot about me, the work I do and about Past Life Regression. The feature came out on August 5th, 1995 (and I was to have my own show on August 5th, 1996 as you will see!). Many months later Paul revealed to me that in September 1991 he had a dream. He dreamt that he went to see a fortune teller. He went through a door where there was a bed behind the door covered in sparkling Indian fabric (exactly like my bedroom). There, standing in the middle of the room, was a "wooden" statue offering him a pink rose, and yes — the wooden statue was of Marilyn Monroe, a madonna dressed in a shimmering white chiffon dress.

Now Paul, who claimed not to be psychic until now (I always see his grandfather in Spirit by his righthand side) has found this more than just coincidence. (There are no such things as coincidences. Coincidences all have a purpose. They come for a reason, good or bad, for our spiritual growth.)

The other thing is that Marilyn passed into Spirit in the early hours between the 4th and 5th of August, 1962. Paul's feature about me came out on August 5th, 1995. The very date that Marilyn was found — but in 1962, of course. There has to be a great significance with all this happening and obviously Marilyn knew (and it was destiny through divine Spirit intervention) that Paul and I were meant to meet. Way back in September of 1991, when Paul had his dream, Marilyn was making contact and communicating even then.

'She will come through to you and tell you *her* story,' another medium, who knew nothing of this, once said. So far she has and I already know a lot about Marilyn that the world does not know, including details about her death. No matter what happens, I will not reveal anything to the world just yet and no amount of money will talk me into doing so. I have not told anyone, not even my closest friends. I will only tell all when I am given the "go ahead", the o.k. from Marilyn and from Spirit. (Marilyn has also come through to world famous medium Stephen O'Brien while he was travelling in a train.) There's only one thing I will say about what she once said to me:

'I'm sick of it. You would think my death was the only thing that mattered. But I'm glad it happened when it did.'

Since then messages have been given to a friend of mine: the same names and descriptions of rooms, etc. The things described to Pete from Marilyn were exactly the same. He just sat in my front room and told me what came to him. I have not, hand on heart, discussed with him my own crystal clear messages. Until she is ready, let's give the constant enquiring and research into her death a miss. Let's give it a rest until Spirit decide otherwise and let's remember her words to me:

'I'm glad it happened when it did.'

VIVA MARLENE

I remember that May night, don't you, Mother? It was a dark, cold night and I was outside in the garden, gazing at the stars. Suddenly, for no reason whatsoever, Miss Marlene Dietrich flashed in and rested on my mind. 'I must get my crystal ball,' was all I could think. Didn't know why. I did as my intuition guided me to do and gazed into my crystal ball. I gazed and gazed .... and gazed. Nothing. Absolutely nothing. I couldn't understand it.

The next day the world awoke to the news headlines that read 'Marlene Dietrich has passed away'.

It's about time we had a bit more mirth — after all, I am the "Happy Medium"!

I recently did a reading for a new up-and-coming medium named Sandra Field who knows nothing of the aforementioned story. Meaning to say to her, 'Does your husband ever try to re-charge your human aura?', I must have been a bit confused (to say the least) when I came out with:

'When was the last time your husband *charged up your aura*?'

Now, that has a totally new meaning, doesn't it!

To get back to the story:

The next afternoon it's pouring with rain and I'm in your old bedroom, Mother, tidying up a bit. I thought, 'I really ought to go through some of your old books kept in a box under the bed.'

I pull out this box and then, right at the bottom, what do I find? A souvenir programme of Marlene Dietrich, live at the Alexandra Theatre in Birmingham! You went to see her live on stage on May 14th, 1973 and I never knew. If you told me, then why can't I remember? I got cross at first, thinking, 'Why didn't you tell me?' It's quite a thing to say you saw Marlene Dietrich live on stage and something most people would talk about for the rest of their lives. But you didn't, Mother. You never said a word. Now that I've given it some thought, I know why. It was something you wanted to do for *you.* Something personal. We all deserve to do something personal and special for ourselves sometimes, don't we? Oh, I'm so glad you did. I'm so glad you did something for you!

Next day the postman knocks on the door with a parcel addressed to: Mystic Ed. Do not bend (oh, yes, he does!). I open it. It's from Sandra Field. I read her letter. It begins:

Dear Ed,

I suppose by now you are wondering what I'm doing sending you a gift pertaining to Marlene Dietrich. I couldn't resist sending this picture postcard of her. Strange sort of gift. Any ideas?

I think Sandra is going to be a good medium, don't you?

DIANA DORS — MY MOONLIGHT MADONNA

Diana appeared to me in my front room the evening before my first appearance on BBC Radio WM on the Rustie Lee show. There she stood, as beautiful as ever — even more — in powder-blue chiffon and wearing the D.O.R.S. necklace. Before she appeared, the smell of perfume — Ma Griffe — filled the air. She chatted away and gave me messages — important messages — to give one day to Freddie Starr (personal to Freddie only — sorry!). I have a cassette of hers called "Swingin' Dors" and driving to the BBC with

Gabriela the next day we thought we'd play it in the car. It just wouldn't play properly. Too fast, too slow, all distorted until we had to switch it off.

I found out later that on the week Diana passed over she should have been in the very same studios. No wonder she came along that day! Well, Diana is wonderful now. More beautiful than she ever was. I call her my Moonlight Madonna.

I have to admit that I am at times moved to tears to think that such great names have made themselves "known" to me and yet they are all in Spirit, as we will all be one day. When they were on this earth plane they were humans with feelings just like ourselves. Whether people in Spirit were once rich, poor, famous or otherwise, we must remember that their earthly cycles are completed. They have moved on to the higher realms with greater knowledge, love and wisdom than we have here on earth and they can choose to contact any one of us. But only when, if and who *they* choose. That choice is left to the person in Spirit. They know what the true value of life is. And we mustn't forget that Spirit have a wonderful sense of humour. It's not all doom and gloom "up there".

If it was, why do you think they've stayed on for so long? ....

I dare say some people will say, 'Those stars are getting through to *him*!' and I'm prepared for the knocks, the mockery and the laughter. But I don't care. These things have really happened to me and I thank God for them. Everyone is a celebrity in the world of Spirit and each one of them a Star!

God bless all of you!

IV

Spring, 1996

Dear Mother,
Time's flying past. I'm still making appearances on radio. Wish they would pay me for once. I still have to pay the gas bills, etc.! Another call from BBC Radio Shropshire today: 'It's Elvis Day tomorrow, Mystic — can you come on the programme and bring Elvis with you?'

Well, I can't do that! It really doesn't work that way.

Went on the show and pretended to be Priscilla Presley. Did a reading on air pretending to be her and turned over the tarot cards. Strange how the King of Swords came up! Swords are all to do with communication and after all, Elvis was a singer. And wasn't he called the King? So in a way I did bring him with me.

Chapter Eleven

Easter, 1996

Dear Mother,

Oh, Mother! Just when life was going well .... Remember Jock? Remember me lending him money to pay off his debts — money you left me? Remember how he never tried to pay me back? Yes, I know he did promise, but he didn't try, did he? Remember how I used to walk around in the middle of the night with my head in my hands, wondering how on earth I was going to pay my *own* bills? I can remember feeling so angry with myself at the time of lending it to him because he didn't offer to pay me back. I felt I had gone against your wishes. For God's sake, that money was to help me! Remember how he even lent some of it to a friend for a foreign holiday?

Jock has been staying with me for months now. I've been trying to get him to love himself and forgive himself. Stayed up some nights until three in the morning with him and yet I keep saying, 'I know there's something you're not telling me.'

'No, there's not.'

My intuition is telling me otherwise. I don't have to be psychic to know that he's about to spit out something. Well, whatever it is I wish he would do it soon ....

He's in such a depressed state I've just got to keep my eyes on him. He seems to have no interest in life in any way. I've had to not discuss money with him right now. I don't want to rub salt into the wound. Why he's acting like this, I just don't know. I only know I've got to get him back into shape again. Money isn't everything. His friendship means more. I just want to see him smile again and enjoy life.

I'd had my first break without him being here this evening, Maundy Thursday. He's gone to see his aunt. I've been listening to you playing Rachmaninov by candle-light tonight, Mother. I feel the presence of Spirit stronger than I have for a long, long time. As though I've got a house full. It's wonderful. (My friend from Spirit's here. He wants me to call him George.) Oh, you played the piano so beautifully, Mother. With this tape you have left me a wonderful legacy.

Oh, that's the doorbell. Jock's returned. He looks upset. Still sitting in candlelight he looks at me. I look at him.

'What ....?'

'I've something to tell you, Ed. You're not going to be very pleased.'

'Oh God, Jock. I feel a fag coming on.'

I reach for a cigarette and light it. There's a strange, awesome and mysterious silence in the room.

'Ed, you know that money you lent me to pay my bills off with ...?'

'Spit it out.'

'You're not going to like it.'

'For crying out loud, tell me what it is — now!'

'That money for my unpaid bills .... I've .... well .... I spent it ....'

I feel a knife has been driven into my heart. I bury my face in my hands. I feel I could pull my hair out by the roots. He spent your money, Mother. I might as well have thrown it out into the road or at least given it to charity. Or even spent it on myself and been able to pay my bills on time. Jock tells me he's sorry. My head's spinning. I either kill him, send him out of my life right now — or forgive him.

'You *bastard!* You absolute idiot! Why didn't you pay off your bills?'

'I thought I could get away with it. I'm sorry, really I am. They've caught up with me, you see. The debt collectors. The bailiffs. I'm really sorry.'

All that money gone. Gone on drinks down at the pub. Wasted on rubbish. The money I shouldn't have ever touched unless it was for a real emergency.

'It's not the money, Jock. It's *me* you've used. You've used my friendship and loyalty and the love I had for you. All this time, all these months getting you to love yourself! I've needed a holiday. I haven't had one for ten years or more. Yet you gave nearly £400 of my money to someone else so they could have one! How could you take from me and use me in this way?'

Jock suddenly bursts into tears. I want to smack him really hard for treating me like this and for chucking your money down the drain, Mother. I feel I'm going to kill him — any minute now! And then ....

He cries. I get up. Take him in my arms. I know from his tears how truly sorry he is. He's also sorry that it's all caught up with him. He's sorry for using me and treating me like he has, but he's also sorry for himself. Because he's been found out. Caught up with.

Where do we go from here? I ask myself.

'My aunt's going to pay you back and pay off all my debts,' sobs Jock.

This time I shan't refuse repayment. I feel so very sorry for her, having to part now with her hard-earned money.

'I'll forgive you, Jock,' I say. 'But I will never forget it.'

FORGIVENESS

While writing this — money returned or not — I still can't get over it. Yet we've all done things in life we are not proud of. If we don't learn how to forgive, how can we expect to be forgiven? If I don't forgive him, I will only hold hate and resentment within my heart. Jock has learnt from his mistakes, like we all do. He has a new job now and is putting things right again. I wish him a happy life. In many ways I have also learnt lessons.

Maybe I was the one who made a mistake by helping him in the first place, when his family should have done so. Yet he didn't want them to be ashamed of him. That's why we kept it between ourselves.

Jock and I will always be friends — in this life and in the next one. Like with every experience in life, it's about learning and growth. Once you've gone through the pain of that experience you become stronger and wiser. Able to help others who come to you and who have gone through similar events. It's all part of life's rich tapestry. After the storms, the rainbow of hope shines through.

To Brian and Sue I give grateful thanks for giving me shelter from the storm. For giving me a place to rest my troubled mind at the end of that experience, when I couldn't take any more. When I needed peace of mind. They gave me that peace and the strength and support to carry on.

You know, Mother. I know that people reading this book and the experiences within it will be able to associate them with this own lives. Let's hope that the messages from this book will help many people to never give up. Whatever life throws at you, be strong. Forgive. Love and believe in yourself. Thank God for this precious gift of life.

Spirit will always see you get through in the end. If you find that trust is shaken by people on this earth, then believe in Spirit. They will never let you down.

II

May, 1996

Dear Mother,

You know, Mother darling, so many people have lost all their families and have no one. We have all been destined to meet our "second families", the ones chosen for us to meet along this highway in life. When we start again with our lives we need direction, guidance. We start out on a fifty thousand mile journey which begins with the first step. Once we take that first step, go out into the world again and start to *give* to others, all the right people meant to come into our lives at the right moments in time do so. We have to open the gates of heaven within our hearts and let others in.

My second family consists not only of Gabriela, Brian and Susan, Steve, but also the "crew" at Solstice in Bridgnorth and all the wonderful people I have met through them. On each spare moment I had I went over to Bridgnorth just to be with them — such very special people in my life who I'm proud to have as my very best and truest friends. All of them mentioned do not care whether I'm rich, poor, famous or otherwise. They love me for me, believe in me and I love them all individually more than words can say. The crew of Solstice are all givers in a world of takers. They all have rare and special qualities. A beautiful radiant light shines and glows from all of them and they touch people's lives every day by just being themselves. Just by bringing happiness and joy deep into the hearts of all they meet in their day-to-say activities. There's "Ray-of-Sunshine" Ray and his wife Bridget, the beauty of Bridgnorth; there's talented pianist Val and Dave, her husband. There's gorgeous Julie, whose spiritual beauty glows outwards from within her and her lovely husband Harry, who sends out healing energy to all. Then there's Beth and Martin, Lou Jack and Nula — all who I'm proud to have as my friends. This letter to you, Mother, wouldn't be complete without mentioning Julie's adopted son Pete. He's a man with a giant plectrum, he's a giant keyboard of sensuality and a man with a musical bent! A true friend and Cancerian who has great talent with his songwriting. I know he will make it big in the world of music, so we must all listen for the name Pete Simpson. Based on a romantic interlude of mine he was inspired to write a beautiful song called "One Step Closer to Love". There are so many people to mention here! I hope some of them will not be disappointed or offended if they haven't been included. To think, Mother, that when you passed into Spirit I had few friends. Certainly few who cared for me. Yet now there are so many who I thank God, the world of Spirit and you, Mother, for sending to me. My second family. So many true friends. There is Sandy, Gerald, Anita, Sandra, Paul, Alexis, Dolores — so very many wonderful "brothers and sisters" who I am so proud of. I love you all so much.

Such a shame about the many takers, users and drainers I was yet to meet ....

III

June 1st, 1996

Dear Mother,

It is so important that people keep a dream book by their beds. We re-live so many stresses that build up during the day through our dreams and our greatest psychic foresight comes through. We easily go back in time through our dreams, which is also why so many people feel drained upon waking in the morning and also by having outer body experiences throughout the night. When we sink into deep sleep it is nothing new for our spiritual bodies to become disconnected from our physical bodies. While our physical bodies rest in sleep, our spiritual selves can travel all over the place and there is nothing to fear from this.

(When I have an astral projection I often wake up to find I've been halfway up Ben Nevis .... Another happy medium joke — well, nearly!)

Remember that we are indeed made up of two forces, the physical and the spiritual. There are many people, and I know of one or two who do this, who will focus their attention upon other people, "astrally project" over to where these people live and can actually watch what others are doing. Personally I feel that this, like with every psychic and spiritual gift, should only be done with a) the other person's permission or b) should the other person require another to keep an eye on them if they happen to be experiencing problems within their own lives.

Basically, to "travel" into another's bedroom, for example, is unfair and an invasion of someone's privacy — and without someone's consent is completely in the wrong. As said earlier, I have been visited astrally by others who are just "trying things out" and this is when it can become dangerous to them. Nowadays there are plenty of books on outer body experiences and astral projection. A full comprehension of these subjects needs to be understood and recognised before carrying out such practices.

Very often psychics can feel as if they are being elevated upwards during meditation. We have to remember that during these periods our vibrations are raised by our guides to prepare us for spiritual work, so again there is nothing to fear. My personal feelings are that no one should dabble with things they don't understand. We must study seriously psychic/spiritual matters, putting protection around ourselves against harmful influences from this world or the next, remembering to "open up" and "close down" appropriately before undertaking any form of psychic work.

I myself feel very protected by Spirit and these feelings will come about if you wish to help others with the gifts you have been given from God and from Spirit. All mediums should, I feel, work together in love and in their own ways to help others. There should not be jealousy, animosity, hate or any ill feeling if one medium is more successful than another. We should all thank God and the world of Spirit for helping a very successful medium to get on well. If they are jealous and happen to make sarcastic comments, they themselves are not working "with love" and obviously want recognition. We all have the chance to be recognised for the work we wish and are required to do for Spirit. If it is our destiny to have our name in lights, it will be so. O.k., I've been on radio/TV and in local and national press, but the people I have met and been able to help as a result is what it's all about. To still be on a one to one basis at the end of the day means everything to me when I can be alone with someone to show that there is light at the end of the tunnel and that they do have hope for the future. I suppose I do see myself in many ways as being a guide and a listening ear for many people who are lost or need a shoulder to cry on, living as we do in a world of people who won't spare the time to listen. It is very sad. To sum up, I suppose this is where I fit in.

I have to admit, though, that there are people who will suck you dry of all your energy if you let them and people who will phone you time and time again, not just to talk (I don't mind that when people have a serious problem, you can save someone's life that way), but to keep on with:

'What are you picking up?'

'Can you remember what you told me last June?'

'I know it's 2 in the morning, but I've just bought a crystal ball. Can you tell me how to use it, please?'

Or even worse:

'Can you *phone* me *back* and tell me how to read the cards?' etc. etc.

It's at times like these when I have to let people know that I need my own space to restore and recharge my batteries and also to get sleep! If I didn't I would never have time to be me, wash my socks, iron my boxers, rest, do my book-keeping and beside which — I would be totally drained, unable to help anyone who needed serious help the next day. Plus I would have (and have had in the past) a terrible phone bill!

IV

June, 1996

Dear Mother,

I'm going on BBC radio again tomorrow, darling, and I don't want to do it! For many years now I've needed someone in my life to want me for *me*. Spiritually, yet with a physical expression. The cards told me not to build my hopes up. Wish I'd taken their advice now. You see, someone came into my life recently. It was what I had been waiting for. But I've found out that it's not meant to be and the cards did tell me ....

The physical side of my life had been non-existent for many years, so to "give in" seemed right and wrong all at the same time. Basically because I live such a spiritual way of life and always felt that anything physical could spoil things somehow. Yet I/we have to remember that we're only human and have been given and blessed with desires that are natural and need to be expressed. I allowed my heart to be broken. I saw it all in the cards and another prediction came true. How can you possibly blame someone for something that you yourself foresaw?

In my hour of need I drove to Wales. Didn't tell anyone I knew, just went. We had had a tremendous thunderstorm that evening and I shall never forget standing looking out at sea, the angry tormented sea just like my heart, and watching the lightening flashing viciously across a purple velvet sky. The tears rolled down my face. Oh, the pain! I fell in love and then it was over ....

Oh, when will someone really fall in love with me? Maybe it's not meant. Not yet, anyway. I spend such a great deal of my life bringing people together in love, so to want someone of my own surely can't be that selfish. We all need *one* person in our lives who can be our rock and our foundation.

I know, Mother, that many people reading this will understand my feelings without saying, 'He's psychic, he should've known better!' Understand how deeply that knife cuts into the heart after love has gone away.

(I shall always love that person until the end of time and hope they too find that someone special who will love them equally as much as I do.)

None of my closest friends knew who that person was, but they did comment at the time on how the love had gone from my eyes. My motivation for life was gone. No interest. So many wonderful things had happened since your passing, Mother, and I've met so many good and trustworthy friends, but at this moment in time nothing matters. Nothing matters at all.

Driving back from Wales in the early hours of a stiflingly hot summer morning I feel a hand from Spirit — whose, I don't know — rest upon my shoulder. And then a voice says: 'It's o.k. You'll pull through. We (Spirit) love you. Don't reproach yourself. Let go of the guilt that doesn't belong to you. For now continue to give love to everyone spiritually just like before. Nothing has changed. We're here for you always. When it is the right time for you, you will meet that person. It was yet another lesson for you to experience. To understand. So you can help others.'

That person didn't know how much they had hurt me by going away. I hold no resentment. I just shouldn't have let it happen .... Wasn't their fault .... I've been such a fool! I'm not wearing your wedding ring, Mother. I don't feel proud enough to wear it. I'm so sorry, Mother. I have only myself to blame and feel I've let you down ....

V

Following morning, June 1996

Dear Mother,

I had the most wonderful dream about you last night. I opened my eyes and just for a second you were standing there, right by the bed. I'm wearing your ring and I'm going to give the performance of my life today. I've put your wedding ring back on and this time it stays on. I've got a good feeling about today!

Well, Mother, stayed on radio today on and off for about three hours. The producer, Mary Fox, let me announce that my own show, called "Mystic Ed-lines", is coming soon to BBC Radio Shropshire!

Just think: if I'd driven off to Wales and not returned, this wouldn't have happened. I predicted I would have my own show and many people said, 'How do you think you're going to do *that*?' Well, Spirit have obviously been on my side, pushing me on in the face of adversity and criticism because they all know how much I want to work for and with them. I don't want this "fame" thing for me. I want it for them. All those lost souls out there that need me as a channel, so I can communicate and give their messages out to the people who need them. Those who feel that the bond has broken and in fact that bond has grown stronger. Yes, of course I get a great buzz from it all! Who wouldn't? It's good for the morale, but it's what I can achieve for others by being on radio/TV (and what was still yet to happen — a live audience).

I even received a call on air from a lady who had just been through exactly the same experience as myself romantically and guess what? That's right! I knew exactly how she felt and I had the right words to say to her. To give her hope. Give her back control of herself and for her to love herself again. My heartbreaking experience had been sent to me for a purpose. I was meant to suffer for the benefit of others. After all, how can we *know* how others feel if we haven't had experiences the same as them?

VI

June 29th, 1996

Dear Mother

I'm forty today, Mother. They do say life begins then. Stayed with Brian and Susan and we went to Glastonbury. A fabulous day, but what we didn't anticipate was that over 5,000 people go on a pilgrimage through the streets of Glastonbury on the last Saturday of June every year. It was certainly a spiritual experience! All churches join forces singing hymns as they progress along .... One priest even had his handbag on fire!

'You didn't know that they'd be singing hymns for your birthday, did you?' laughed Sue and Bri. Of course one couldn't get near Glastonbury Abbey, but Brian and I did climb to the top of the Tor. In gale force winds as well. We had a job to stand up in the strong wind, but once inside the Tor it was like a vacuum. When you stand on top of that hillside a great spiritual feeling overcomes you and the Tor is said to be one of the most powerful places in England. I know I have to go there again, hopefully when there aren't so many other tourists. You look over the countryside and face the land of Camelot. Halfway down Brian and I found a bench to rest and meditate. I was aware of a tall man in Spirit standing on the hillside, looking out to the land of Camelot. I believe that this man was Merlin. I walked over to where he stood, but he was gone. A large raven flew over, circled the top of the Tor — and was gone. A strange, yet wonderful Spiritual experience.

Strange to get to my 40th birthday and not feel your presence, Mother. Obviously you knew I was in good company. I still miss you. Nothing has changed there. I would give anything to have you back again.

'If anything every happens to me, you'll have to get yourself a cat for company,' you once told me.

So when my darling Gabriela walked in with a beautiful tabby pussy it was even like a gift from you. First he was called Pharoah, then Merlin and finally Grimoire (meaning a book of Magic). He's called Grimmy for short and it's a marriage made in Heaven. Wherever I go, he goes too.

Chapter Twelve

July, 1996

Dear Mother,

This is going to sound like the great "I am" again, but I've got to tell you what people are asking me to do a lot lately. Bless them. Yes, actually bless them! It got me thinking about how when two people are friends/lovers, I can join them together. Not as in marriage, but as part of the universe so that their love and friendship will remain loyal to each other and will grow and remain with them as long as they live in this world, continuing even into the next life. Definitely a kind of spiritual marriage. It is a really moving experience. A feeling of love floods through our hearts, through our minds — in fact, through our whole being. A euphoria of energy fills the atmosphere. I know Spirit are with us then.

'Love is the Secret of Life.'

I also am asked to hold objects: i.e. jewellery, photographs, crystals, pendulums, etc., so that I can energize them and send loving healing energy to their owners.

I know that one of the greatest gifts I have been given is to give love to others and to take away their burdens.

There have been many wonderful spiritual experiences that I have had lately, especially during this month of July. I went to Buildwas Abbey in Shropshire with a lovely friend named Sandy. Together we were standing in a ruined chapel when we both felt the presence of Spirit. I felt a monk in Spirit either side of me as though we all stood in prayer together. Sandy and I then drove to Much Wenlock where I had never been before, yet felt that I had got to go. Today of all days, for some reason.

Wenlock Abbey ruins give you that feeling of spirituality you cannot explain. A feeling of peace and power all at the same time. The funniest thing was that there were actors in costume rehearsing for "that Scottish play" by Shakespeare. I said to Sandy: 'Oh, look — I said you would meet a knight in shining armour soon! In fact, there's a whole crowd of them over there .... there's even one for me!' as I gazed at one very handsome gentleman whose sword sparkled in the watery sunlight. 'Well, I never — Sandy, it's my Sir Lancelot! Shall you be Guinevere or shall I?'

We had a stroll — Sandy and I, that is — around the grounds. We came across a circular stone building and I went inside it. I removed my pendulum from its black velvet pouch and dowsed. Nothing happened! I joked: 'I'm probably standing inside some kind of mediaeval toilet.'

Sandy laughed. When I got home that evening Sandy had left a message on my machine, laughing all the way through it.

'You were right, Ed — ha ha ha! I've been .... ha ha ha! .... reading the leaflet we bought .... ha ha ha! .... you were standing inside .... ha ha! .... the GENT'S LAVATORY!

I felt all *flushed*!

Earlier that day, after the lavatorium expedition, we went back to where the actors were rehearsing.

'I feel I've got to, Sandy. As though it's meant. Someone there needs some energy.'

A voice called out through the gentle breeze, 'Mystic ....'

I looked puzzled. It was Lady Macbeth herself calling me!

'Mystic! It's me — Sonia!'

It was Sonia Green, a presenter from BBC Radio Shropshire who was dressed as Lady Macbeth. What a small, yet strange and wonderful world we live in! She came over to me and before I could even ask her she said, 'I need some energy fast!'

I held her hand and took out my pendulum.

'We haven't time!' she exclaimed.

'Yes, you have.'

I brought some energy from myself, from Spirit and from all corners of the universe into the pendulum and into her hand. Then I asked her to take all this energy into herself. I felt I had again served my purpose that day. Done my good deed. Then Sandy and I left. A lovely lady is Sandy. Everybody loves her. She is one of life's givers. I hope that she realizes just how many of us love her for being that special person she is.

II

July, 1996

Dear Mother,

I dream of going to Egypt! I know you can soon spend what little money you have on holidays because after all, bills are really more important. But there's this feeling within me that one day I will have to go. I know after being regressed by Brian that I was there in a previous life. I have this burning desire to go in this life. Oh, well. Perhaps one day I will be able to afford to go. I've got my passport ready just in case!

I've had other spiritual experiences lately, sending earthbound spirits into the Light. Especially with different people who have met me and have unknowingly left their so-called deceased with me. So I have had the duty to perform to re-assure those souls that have been hanging on here that it is now time to leave. To go into "the Light". I recall one beautiful experience at Lilleshall Abbey ruins in Shropshire one evening with Brian. Three monks were still "hanging on" to the memories of their lives at the Abbey.

They knew it was time for them to leave. I was "told" to do this. I was aware of three of them with me.

'Who were the *five* you were with?' commented Brian afterwards.

Again, another spiritually rewarding day.

A lovely lady named Carole Walker from Staffordshire County Council has phoned me. I'm going to call her Crystal Carole. Wants me to do a talk at the end of October. I've met Carole and she's gorgeous. A dark-haired beauty who feels that she has had to contact me. She wants to do a lot of PR work for me relating to the talk that she has asked me to do. Normally I've had to do all my own PR work, be my own agent and manager. Many mediums have said that a woman will do this and I have the strangest feeling that when the time comes I will not need to look any further. (I was later to find that regarding preparations for my talk, she was to give one hundred percent of her time and energy.) Crystal Carole deserves to get on.

III

Last week in July, 1996

Dear Mother,

Really must get cracking now on my show, "Mystic Ed-lines" for BBC Radio Shropshire. Got to get guests for the whole week. Got to think what I'm going to talk about. I've never been lost for words before! I want to make the show light, serious, filled with jokes and yet the whole point, I feel, is to give hope to the listeners. That there can always be light at the end of the tunnel. They're not paying me to do the show, unfortunately. This time, though, it's a chance not to miss out on.

What has touched my heart more than anything lately, Mother, has been the distances that people have been prepared to travel just to see me. Oxfordshire, Shropshire, London, Wales (Caernarvon), Germany and — would you believe it? Australia! Recently I've received calls from Barcelona, Spain, from someone who just wished to talk to me. I'm obviously doing something right!

IV

August 4th, 1996

Dear Mother,

Well, it's tomorrow! O.k., it's only a "Summer Special Spotlight Feature", but it is my first taste of my own show with my own guests. I'm ready. The adrenalin's pumping .... Yes, I'm definitely ready now. Hope I don't oversleep on my first day!

Susan has been telling me to get an out-of-print book called *Winged Pharaoh* by Joan Grant. She knows I'm going to get it. Can't think how or why myself. Joan Grant wrote her books in the thirties as novels based on her own past life experiences in Egypt. The strange thing is that I walked into a secondhand bookshop and was able to get my hands on three: *Winged Pharaoh, So Moses was Born* and *The Eyes of Horus.* (Even stranger was that after thirty years or more the little bookshop closed down only a week later!)

This evening, Sunday 4th August, after getting prepared for my big week, I opened the cover of *The Eyes of Horus.* Inside I read an inscription: *With Love to Albert, from Florrie. August 4th, 1945.*

August 4th! Exactly fifty-one years to the date. An uncanny but wonderful feeling flooded me. Today is Albert's birthday — yet I know that whoever he is, Albert is in Spirit now.

Happy Birthday, Albert! I've lit a pure white candle especially for you. I know you're with me this evening. I will treasure your book forever.

We must always remember to light a candle to those we love who are in Spirit as a token of our love and affection for them. That we still remember them.

Fancy owning Albert's book — on his birthday! And they say things can just be coincidence! I don't think so somehow, do you?

Isn't life wonderful! Oh, how I wish you were here with me now, Mother .... I've got to remember that you've helped me to achieve all these things that have happened so far and this so I can work for the world of Spirit.

Chapter Thirteen

August 5th – 9th, 1996

Dear Mother,

Day One –

Strange day, this! Exciting, exhilarating! Strange twist of fate here: exactly a year ago I was a guest on Rustie Lee's Radio WM show and now she's the first "link up" guest on mine. What a tremendous start and what a wonderful interview.

Today is also the anniversary of Miss Monroe's passing into Spirit. Reporter Paul Kemp has also been a guest and we discussed my — and his — Marilyn Monroe story. It is exactly a year since Paul's feature came out about me in the local press, when I was quoted as saying that I would have my own radio or TV show. Today it has come true.

Day Two –

'But you don't swallow essential oils, do you, Julie?'

'No, Ed. I think we'd better make that clear!'

Beautiful Julie! What a lovely interview with her taking me around Solstice, my second home. Julie certainly knows a thing or two about the spiritual way of life.

Next interview: Brian.

'I've got the largest, shiniest crystal balls in the business, Brian.'

'I know — and they sparkle!' was his witty reply. (Wonder how he knows? Must be psychic or something!)

It was a really interesting interview with him about hypnotherapy. Let's hope that people listening in have a better understanding of it now and realize that it's safe and beneficial. That it helps get rid of fears, phobias and help to release pent-up emotions from way back in this life and from other lives so that a person being held back by these things can move forward.

Day Three –

Lovely Sheila Eveson Corbett. She's a cross between Marlene Dietrich and Evelyn Laye. I predicted a year before that she would have some of her magnificent poems published — and they were! I recall her telling me that when I did her a reading in 1995 how she was so excited by the news that afterwards she drove home from her nearby supermarket and then realized that her shopping was still in the trolley!

Same thing happened on the morning of the show. Sheila came to my home so we could drive to the BBC together. Halfway along the motorway she exclaims, 'I don't believe it! *I don't believe it!* I've done it again!'

'Done what again, darling?'

'I've left all my poems, songs and musicals at your house!'

'Never mind. Calm down. We can't go back now. You'll remember them all. Your poems are all safely stored in your mind.'

'Oh, I'm ever so sorry, Ed. I feel I've let you down.'

'You haven't let anyone down. Don't worry.'

'You're so calm about it, Ed.'

'I know. I'm not worried. I believe in you, Sheila. You will remember.'

Sheila, God bless her, *did* remember every word of an outstanding poem about a seagull. It was beautifully said and is a poem no one could easily forget. She's still going places. I know she'll get her plays, poems and musicals in print and performed. Never give up, Sheila. One day it will happen for you when it is meant to. At the right time. The chosen time.

Next interview: Paul, an up-and-coming medium who has been blessed with great gifts of psychometry and transfiguration. I predict he will give a lot of people guidance and hope together with his great faith in God. I wish him every success with his development.

BBC Radio Shropshire have asked me today to make a live appearance next week at the Shrewsbury Flower Show. Isn't that a strange thing, Mother? Year in, year out, we always said that we would go there and never did. Now I am going alone — but am I? I have a wonderful feeling that you will be there by my side. I've decided to "probe" Margaret Thrower (daughter of the late famous gardener Percy Thrower) with my microphone. Bet she'll love that!

Well, I'm halfway through the show now, Mother. Things have gone well and there's been some excellent write-ups about it in the local press. It's funny to read all about oneself when the newspapers arrive. The other day I was going to throw one out, until it fell open and — there I was! I've been extremely risqué on the air. It's a wonder I haven't had a complaint! You know the ones: 'I've got the largest balls in the business' and 'Would you like me to spread them on the table for you?' Will have to tone them down a bit with jokes like:

'What is a medium's favourite roll?'

'Egg and Cress!'

Have received calls from listeners-in. Like:

'You've really done me the power of good!' and, more importantly, 'Now I really believe in life after death. That there is no death. Only life and nothing to fear about going into it.' *That* is what I really want to get over to people. My mission at this time.

Day Four –

First guest: 'She's got the mind of Catherine Cookson, the eyes of Lorna Doone and the lips of Elizabeth Taylor .... She's bold, she's beautiful .... She's Brenda Whincup!'

Lovely Brenda, who I predicted would have a book-signing within twelve months, is now chatting live on air about it and how she is going to do a book-signing at Shrewsbury Abbey in November with the publication of her wonderful book, *Signs of Life*. (If it hadn't been for meeting Brenda, I wouldn't have met my publisher Diana and this book wouldn't have ever been written!)

I know that whatever she writes, Brenda's mother is by her side in Spirit and whoever she dedicates a book to, it's her mother who really gets the dedication. Every time one of Brenda's books are (and will be) published, Brenda's mother gets the credits. Like me, Brenda wants her mother to be proud of her — and she certainly is that! She's just told me so herself while I am writing this chapter. You've got another ten volumes to get through, Brenda — then you can have a rest!

My final guest on "Mystic Ed-lines" was Pete Simpson, the songwriter. He is certainly a man who is going places! Everyone believes that he will make the big time in the world of music. He certainly has got a gift for lyrics, the words of his songs come from his dreams and he also has a tremendous singing voice. He is very gifted spiritually and picks up on good and bad vibrations very quickly. He has a great sense of humour and when on air live I said to him, 'I've got another prediction for you — you're going to write me a song. It's the Mystic Ed theme song,' he laughed out loud. Even I couldn't think why!

The following night at a party he said, 'Do you know why I laughed?'

I looked puzzled. Then he handed me a tape, "One Step Closer to Love". I had inspired him to write a song.

It's the final day tomorrow, Mother. I've got to make it the best performance of my life. It's a live tarot "phone-in". I've tried my best to give our messages for the world of Spirit all week, but tomorrow it's all or nothing. I want people to really sit up and listen. I've given out a lot of ideas to people on air to help them feel confident and I've cracked loads of jokes — well, after all, when you call yourself the "Happy Medium" you've got to live up to it. Tomorrow will be a different thing altogether.

The Final Day –

Pouring with rain, Mother. One of those days that makes you realise that summer is reaching its end. Like the final day of the show, I guess. Coincidences, coincidences .... All those coincidences to do with the start of the show. The book once given to Albert dated August 4th and my buying it on August 4th — and now today, August 9th, Dad's birthday. I know he's looking after you in Spirit, Mother. He was waiting for you when you passed over. He was a good man, my dad. Everyone liked Ron. He'd do anything for anybody. Happy Birthday, Dad. Take care of my Mother for me until I join you both. I wonder what you make of all this, Dad? Bet you'd be down at the pub tonight celebrating if you were still here! I'll have a drink in memory of you tonight at the party.

I haven't said much to you lately, have I, Dad?

I suppose it's because there's no need right now. I remember feeling your presence a lot after you first passed over when we lived at the other house. I was born there, remember? Mother and I weren't happy there after you passed on. It wasn't because of that, though. We loved our little house and kept the garden immaculate. No, there were other reasons why we left. I hope whoever lives there now is happier than we were and I hope they feel your protective presence once in a while. I'm sure whoever they are, they know when you're about!...

Well, Mother, it's the final morning and in memory of you I read out Rudyard Kipling's poem *If* because of the huge messages within each verse. I know you were reading it out with me!

After *If* came the live tarot "phone-in". I did about twenty readings and felt Spirit by my side many times while swiftly turning over the cards. I felt the presence of mothers, fathers, husbands .... They all gave me the right words to say.

Strange feelings as the show ended. As I left, the phones were still ringing one after the other. It's really weird to walk away when so many people needed to speak to me.

Felt exhausted to say the least when I got home. So I lay down for a while to get forty winks, but because everything that had been happening all week was going over and over in my mind I never got them.

II

August, 1996

Dear Mother,

Hottest day of the year, Mother, and I'm ready to go live on air again, but this time before crowds inside a huge marquee at the Shrewsbury flower show. "Probed" Margaret Thrower with my microphone as promised (she did enjoy it!) and gave her a card reading live on air. She was amazed at my accuracy. I said that her father Percy was always about and that was why they had won so many competitions. People in Spirit continue to give help and inspiration and will help to encourage us in all things if we put our trust in them. They help us fifty percent as long as we push on with the other fifty percent. I told Margaret how wonderful it was that in all the marquee there were two chairs by her side that were empty. I knew nobody would sit on them because Margaret's father Percy was beside her and you, Mother darling, were beside him.

I was also put to the test on that live debate show.

'I don't know if Mystic Ed really does see Spirit or whether he just imagines these things,' said one guest.

It was then that I put out the thought to Spirit and to God to give me the right words to say as my reply. As the microphone neared my lips my plea for help came:

'There's a lady in a blue and white dress right at the back of the tent,' I began. 'She's with her husband and standing right behind her is .... her mother in Spirit.'

'Is that correct?' Giulia Harding, the presenter, asked the lady in blue and white.

'Yes,' she answered. 'I've always felt my late mother's presence and I knew I wasn't wrong. I've always hoped that someone would say she was with me and that they could see her.'

'And that is why you were meant to be here today, darling,' I said. 'So you would finally get your proof.'

As the microphone moved over to another guest. I looked across at the lady whose mother was still by her side.

'Oh, *thank you*!' she said silently, speaking the words so that no one could hear.

The following afternoon I returned to a demonstration of tarot readings which lasted nearly two hours. People were crammed inside the tent and others were pushing their way to get in. Never in my life had I had so many people "beneath me". Before that, though, I walked around the flower show. All the while I could hear myself saying, 'See, Mother darling? We did get to the flower show together after all ....'

I kept expecting to see you suddenly appear in a beautiful chiffon summer dress, but no. It was something of a day to say the least. I shall never forget the thunderous applause I received after each reading and especially at the end.

So now I do believe that "Mystic Ed-lines" is really over. I can say I had my own show. Now I need a rest!

Viva Gabriela and God bless her for introducing me to the exciting world of Greek yoghurt! I'm eating it with everything and I can't believe why I'm not fat! She's a friend indeed, a lovely friend. My angel from heaven. I shall never forget what love and goodness she has brought into my life. I'll never forget the day the Telegraph magazine came out. There I was in bed when the doorbell rang. I flew out of bed, a vision in flannelette and Mother's pink bedsocks, opened the door to hear Gabriela yell out, 'Party!' — at 7 a.m! Silly string and streamers shot across the hall followed by a champagne cork! She placed in my hand a wand made of tinfoil and placed a party hat on my head! After she was gone I realized that she had decorated *every* shrub in my front garden with Christmas decorations. What a girl! And what special people I have met this year!

I have a great affinity with Ray from Solstice and his beautiful wife Bridget. "Ray-of-Sunshine" Ray is exactly that. He is such a very special person. Everyone who meets him loves him.

He's the man to give you energy
Just when you've gone all flop;
One day he's sure that he'll explode
Just like a bottle of pop!

I know he and I were brothers in a past life and it's like that now. I love him, he's my pal. Bridget is so special because she will *listen,* which so many people don't do nowadays. She has a rare quality of love that is genuine and her intuition of people — good and bad — is always spot on. It's so wonderful to have friends like these. They give so much out to people and I know they're concerned about people using me and putting on me. They are concerned about anyone breaking my heart, too. (Let's hope — next time — my heart won't get broken.) There are so many things to say about Ray and Bridget that could fill a book. Things that are too personal to mention, but there is one thing I can say:

'I love you, Ray, and I love you, Bridget. My love for your will never die. You've done so much for me. You keep *me* loving me. God bless you both.'

Brian, Susan, Sandra Field and Alex .... Oh, what a family I've been blessed with! I've now got my second family and I truly believe that God has sent all of you to me to share laughter, success and tears. How much I love all of you — words can't explain how much! How can I say I'm lonely with such special brothers and sisters? None of us are alone in this life. As long as we have our belief in Spirit, our Guardian Angels and our Spirit Guides we are not alone, none of us. Besides which, we are all part of divine universal energy with our own parts to play in this world, however great or small, finding out every day what our true destinies are. With each learning lesson and with each experience, every day of our lives becomes one of growth and knowledge. We gain strength wisdom and love through every lesson, every hurdle that we get over. We are all meant to be here. As it says in the "Desiderata":

> 'No less than the trees and the stars, you have
> a right to be here. *Strive* to be happy!'

Chapter Fourteen

September, 1996

Dear Mother,

Sometimes I still can't believe you're in Spirit.

I was going through all the photograph albums today, looking for a nice picture of you for this book. I found myself getting quite upset at one stage. We have to remember than when it's "your time to go", it's "your time". Yet looking through the albums I keep remembering different times that were good, bad — all kinds of memories. You were a very misunderstood lady, Mother. People always loved to criticize you, be unkind to you. So now it's time in the book to speak up for you. All those people who used to run you down and pull you to pieces to my face — why did they do it? Jealousy! They were jealous of your looks, your sense of style and your elegant charm. Yet why should they have all been so bitchy, so spiteful? We'll never know. People — mainly women — would mimic your ladylike ways behind your back.

So uncalled for. So unnecessary. There was no need.

You were always there for other people. How many were there for you? You gave up everything to be a wife and mother. We were just like brother and sister when we went out shopping together, weren't we? Had some good times together ....

I dare say you and Violet (Violet Carson, who played Ena Sharples in *Coronation Street*), your friend, are now playing duets in the world of Spirit. You on the piano and she on the organ. Doing what you loved best. After Dad passed on I became your life. So long as I was happy, you were happy. You used to say, 'I don't want you to be lonely when I'm gone.' Because of this you've now made sure I'm not, with all the wonderful friends I now have. But I am lonely for *you*, darling. Dare say you've met Greer Garson, your favourite Hollywood actress, now in Spirit. People mistook you for her, didn't they? You had her elegance and personality, but you were one on your own. I have to keep pushing on now, working with Spirit so you can be proud of me.

'But I am, darling,' I've just heard you say. 'Tell them they are special.'

'Who, Mother?'

'Everyone! Tell them not to let others take away their control. Tell them they are unique. Tell them they are special, just as you are to me.'

'Am I, Mother?'

'You know you are. But you do get lonely without me and you've let people put on you. Don't think I don't know.'

'But people need me, Mother.'

'Not *all* of the time. Give a bit of time to yourself. Have a rest occasionally. You don't have to open the door — and your heart — to everyone you meet. Take time out to smell the roses and to look after those roses planted in the garden of your heart. I will send you a partner soon. You will know who it is when you meet each other. For now, just enjoy your freedom.'

I can now hear Granma's voice:

'I was with you when you were upset. When your heart was broken. You didn't know, did you? Your Mother and I are together — and your Dad. Voice your opinions, because you're starting to shine light into other people's darkness. Other mediums know when I'm about, you know.'

'Do they?'

'Oh, yes. But you're meeting a lot of frauds too. Some of them are crazy. Don't trust all of them or you may find a knife plunged into your back. You can tell Yvonne Pamley that she is to fulfil her mission first. She is a true medium and I have been with you when you have sat together. She is to have another helper soon. Continue to give her hope. I'm with Bob now, you know, and I'm happy. It's a change not to have those pains any more now that I'm in a different place. Ask Phyllis about Sammy ....'

'What about Sammy, Mother?'

'When you and Paul are together, Sammy's been sitting on the knee of his father. Tell him about it. He's preparing his father for spiritual matters. This is why he passed into Spirit. For this reason. Paul is your protector and you are his guide for now. You'll be sad when he's gone, but it's not yet. You're going to find a lot of spiritual development between the two of you. We're all here for you, you know. We're always about. You just don't realize it because we were all so close. But you do feel love emanating out from us, don't you?'

'Oh yes, Mother. I can't see you, but I feel your presence strongly. When will I see you?'

'Not yet. Soon.'

'How soon?'

'We cannot tell you. By the way, you're spoiling that cat!'

Whoops! They're right. I am!

'I miss you, Mother. Granma. Oh, I do miss you!'

'We miss you too,' I hear my mother say, but the voices are now getting quieter and quieter.

'Give Rose-marie our love. She was with you this evening. She gave you a cross to hold carved by Wallace. Send Wallace into the Light. He's hanging on to the past. He needs to be here. He needs to let go and move on.'

'I knew you'd like Rose-marie. She's a very lovely lady. And she is going to be a great healer.'

'Yes, she will be. In fact, she is. Tell her we will send out all the energy she needs — and some happiness. Rose-marie deserves to be happy. Olivia, her daughter, will be a great medium when she grows up. Convince her of this. It's time for us to go now.'

'I don't want you to! Just a little longer?'

'Goodnight, darling ....'

A voice comes from Paul's little boy Sam in Spirit. Softly and gently, yet impatiently, he wants to make sure he gives me his message:

'Tell .... tell my Dad .... tell him I love him ....'

'Of course, Sammy. Don't be sad for your father. I'll tell him you love him and that you're helping him.'

'Thank you.'

Silence. The voices have stopped.

So many people get afraid when they hear voices, but there's no need. If for instance we hear "crying", maybe we should send our love out to that poor soul and ask them what's wrong, what's upsetting them and how we can help them. It may be that they're crying to "make us" hear!

Oh, Mother! There I was writing to you and then you began to talk to me. It's one of the strongest messages of your existence I've had since your passing. It will be two years in November. How my life has changed! It's all thanks to you, all of you in Spirit. Tonight I feel good. Real good! There's something else coming soon .... Something good. I feel my work has only just started.

To all those people who judged, criticized, mocked and ran my mother down:

There was no need and no point. My mother was a good woman who never judged or criticized any of you. My mother had a heart of gold. As it says in the Bible:

'Do not judge and you will not be judged.'

'Any of you who are without sin — cast the first stone.'

It is true, that saying: 'What goes round comes round.'

Who are we, any of us, to judge? Has it made any of you happy to run my mother down? Has it made you better people? I don't think so. How does it make you feel when I put it to you that cancer can be caused from sadness and hurt? The tongue is mightier than the sword! Any of you who persecuted her with harsh words and unnecessary unkindness — I hope that you will one day find peace of mind from all your cruel actions. So on behalf of my mother and myself I am sending out loving, universal energy. May God forgive you and send you his peace.

You were a peacemaker, weren't you, Mother? Always tried to do the right thing. Anyone reading this can think, 'Oh well, he's a mother's boy so he would see no wrong in her.' That is their choice, isn't it, Mother? They can think whatever they like. You and I knew the truth though, didn't we? Still do, but it's all gone now. I have to quote another saying:

'Never speak ill of the dead.'

For if you do — notice a marked change in your life and not for the better, either. You're asking to get yourself HAUNTED! Never doubt the existence of Spirit. There is more power in the realms of Spirit than on this earth plane. You have been warned!

Forgive. Send out love. The same will be returned unto you. That is why giving out love and peace to all we meet in our daily lives is so important:

'Blessed are the Peacemakers'

Wouldn't the world be a better place if every day of our lives we gave someone love, happiness and peace? If we're unable to go out or even are restricted to our beds we can still "send it out" from our hearts and through our communication with Spirit and from God.

Let's all thank God for our lives and the precious gift of life and move forward.

Chapter Fifteen

October, 1996

Dear Mother,

My personal belief in the resurrection of Spirit from the body comes from the story of Christ's own resurrection. Many people hold many views about passing into Spirit. Personally, I believe that when Christ was taken from the cross and then arose three days later *that* was the message of hope to all of us. That our Spirit bodies would also follow that procedure. How can anyone say that there is no such thing as resurrection and the world of Spirit, when Christ proved all this to us? When people say that I am dabbling in something I shouldn't, I always give the same reply:

'Wasn't Jesus the greatest psychic of all time? Wasn't he the greatest spiritual healer? And after all, the Bible is full of prophecy from beginning to end.'

Remember that Jesus Christ "foresaw" his death and his resurrection. He predicted this and it came true. For instance, I myself know that my time will come only when I have completed my own mission. Like Jesus I — in fact, none of us — should be afraid of passing into Spirit. It is, as I've said before, this life on earth that is the test to see how we turn out at the end. Didn't Jesus also say, 'In my Father's house are many mansions'?

Many people reading this, Mother, will no doubt say, 'Oh, here we go again! Someone else claiming to be the son of God.'

But I say to them:

'No! We are *all* the sons of God. We have to follow in the Master's footsteps, giving out love, healing, putting people onto their chosen pathways. Helping them to find the God-spark, which is love, within themselves. Remember in the New Testament that Jesus said, 'The Kingdom of Heaven is within you.'

I also believe that so is the Kingdom of Hell. I'm sure everyone will agree with me in saying that they know which one should win! You don't have to be psychic to realise that. Love conquers all!

I believe that every good gift comes from God and I thank him for the gifts he has given me so I can help others. If I/we don't use these gifts such as healing and guidance, wouldn't that be a terrible waste!

Many people say how psychic I am, yet I disagree because I know *we all* have the ability. All we have to do is to develop our gifts. Laughter and trying to make someone else happy is one of the greatest ways of healing. It's free. It costs nothing to give out to someone and the rewards of, for instance, getting some poor depressed person to smile are worth more than all the gold and silver in the whole world.

II

October, 1996

Dear Mother,

'You are getting famous, aren't you?' asked the lady from my local petrol station today. 'A lady saw you walk out of here the other day and she said to me, "Oh! Was *that* Mystic Ed?" '

Was "mobbed" by a further three ladies in the supermarket earlier today. It's funny autographing someone's shopping list! Then on to the post office ....

'Say a few more words,' said a gentleman in the queue.

'What would you like me to say?'

'That'll do!' he replied. 'It *is* you. Heard you on radio last week and I thoroughly enjoyed it.'

It's getting quite embarrassing. I suppose I'm going to have to get used to it. After all, there's something about me in the local press nearly every week. I'm beginning to realize how really famous people must feel when they can't go anywhere without sun glasses and a wig on! I love it right now, but it can be just a touch annoying, like this evening when I was sitting in the vet's waiting room waiting to get Grimoire inoculated, and people nudge each other and say more than a little loudly, 'Where do I know him from?' It continues with a long, lingering stare until they finally realize where they have seen me before.

I suppose my career in bank robbery is over now!

Seriously, it can be quite exciting and although I'm no mega-star, it adds a touch of spice to what would otherwise be a normal shopping trip, etc. But it does have it's bad side — like with my talk at the library coming up at the end of this month.

Crystal Carole has told me that the talk on the 30th of October is a sell-out, so I've got to do it all again on the 6th of November, which has also sold out! So I've got to make it the best talk yet .... but .... I've had a death threat via the telephone. Apparently the "man" said I'm going to end up with my severed head on top of a lamp-post on the 30th because what I do is evil!

How can getting people to live life to the full through guidance from God and from Spirit be evil? Just shows how little he knows! It also shows how well you're getting on when something like that happens — when people start to hate you.

I'm trying each day to give out so much loving healing energy to people, Mother. So this threat doesn't seem quite fair. Yet this man obviously doesn't know what I'm all about. I am not afraid, but I know that some of my closest friends are worried for me.

They will be at the talk, just in case — yet they're also at the talk because they want to be. Bless 'em! I know that whatever happens, Spirit — and God — will protect me. And I know for certain that you will be by my side, Mother. I feel a great, inexplicable and enormous power within me now — at the moment of writing this — tell me that all is well and I mustn't fear.

III

October, 1996

Dear Mother,

Yet another news item in the local press today about me going going on Beacon Radio for two hours to do a live tarot phone-in. Well, I've just returned home from doing it to find my answering machine filled with messages like:

'Where the *hell* are you? I've been listening for hours and you're not on!'

'Is there anybody there? Are you still alive? I'm really worried about you!'

What I didn't realize was that I was in the Beacon Radio studio, but I ended up on W.A.B.C! So you could say that I've been on the "other side" myself! So I've got to apologize to everyone now. I didn't know! Shame, really, as I gave all my dearest friends a mention to help make their day!

Diana of Blue Dragon needs me to finish writing this volume so it can get printed. Everyone I know wants a copy! Hope they will get a lot of guidance through reading it.

It will be two years in November since you passed over, Mother! Can't believe it. This year the leaves are changing colour just how you would like them. This time of year especially I think of you and your last days on this earth plane. The suffering you went through. I can remember your words as if you have just spoken them:

'May as well *be* dead if I've got to suffer like this ....'

(Good grief! As I wrote that last sentence the lights flashed on and off and on again! I know you're with me tonight.)

I knew in those last days I couldn't stand it much longer. I wanted to cry, but couldn't. Wanted to make you well again, but couldn't. You were being called to Spirit at your chosen time. You fought on so long and finally you were too weak to fight. Too poorly. Yet, thinking back, your illness — like anyone's — was still a short time, however long it went on for, in comparison to the many years of happiness we spent together. All of us who have lost mothers must realize that on their birthdays, Christmas, Mother's Day, etc., those in Spirit are even closer to us then. We all must remember and believe this. They feel even more empathy and love for us at those times.

I know it's you that's pushing me on, Mother. I sense your presence strongly. To guide me into meeting many sad souls who feel that they have lost their loved ones forever. So that I can give them comfort, guidance, counselling and that reassurance that Spirit are with them.

IV

October, 1996

Dear Mother,

The strangest thing happened today that made my hair stand on end. Remember on that terrible night when you passed into Spirit and I was in that large room crying out: 'Where are you *now* when I need you so much!' to someone I once loved? Over twenty years ago it was .... so long ago now.

A gentleman came to see me for a reading this afternoon. He said he remembered me from all those years ago. I didn't recognize him. Before he sat down, he said,

'Do you remember .... (he said the name)?'

'Oh, yes,' I replied. An overwhelming feeling washed over me. I felt a tingling all over my body.

'Well, they're dead!'

We were both sitting down by this time. It's rarely that I am lost for words, but on this occasion I was speechless. Yet something had told me years ago that this person was in Spirit.

'It was a massive heart attack,' my visitor continued. 'They really — and I mean really — were a user, a taker and a destroyer.'

'Was it twelve years ago?' I asked for some unknown reason. (Obviously prompted by spirit communication.)

'About that — yes, it was,' he replied, adding, 'That person hurt a lot of people.'

Didn't I know it! I even stayed away from you on your birthday once, didn't I, Mother. To be with *them.* I know, Mother darling, how hurt you were and I never really forgave myself for that. I was so in love, though. But it ended in heartbreak and I was lucky to be alive because of that person's Jekyll and Hyde character. If I hadn't escaped — falling into your arms in tears, Mother — I wouldn't be alive today. I know that.

And now that person is gone. Now that person is in Spirit ....

I had to act as if the gentleman hadn't told me anything. Shuffled my tarot cards and asked him to cut them so I could do his reading. Positively. Confidently. I had to block what he'd told me out of my mind.

I drove home this evening with so many memories spinning through my mind about that relationship. That first love and the bitter consequences I endured with a pain deep inside my heart that I carried with me for so long. I thought I'd gotten over it. Now it's all come flooding back like a bad dream.

I parked in my driveway and walked into my home, expecting to be alone all evening with these thoughts buzzing inside my mind. I was still in my coat when the doorbell rang. It was my good friend Paul.

'I'm really glad to have company tonight,' I said, 'because I've had a very strange sort of day.'

I told Paul my story. His listened — and understood.

'What must be waiting for someone who hurt and destroyed many lives when they pass into Spirit?' I wondered.

As wise as always, Paul's reply came: 'Well, they know now, my friend. They do know now.'

Many thoughts flashed through my mind about this. We, as humans on this earth plane, do not know all the answers. Maybe they were called to Spirit so they would no longer hurt others? Maybe they repented in their later years? Paul is right. They *do* know now. Everything has been revealed to them. It is important to remember that if we continue to be a taker or a user in this life, that in the next life we may have people use us or take from us. Or maybe — and I personally believe this to be the case — that in our next life we will *give* to others. *Love* them and not hate. To put the karmic debt right and begin again.

Yet I still loved that person. There were good times as well as bad and that horrific end that I cannot write about now. Some things are too personal for the world to know. So I forgive. Better late than never. We have to forgive or we won't be forgiven. We've all done things we shouldn't do, haven't we?

I made Paul and myself a cup of tea and we sat in meditation. I suddenly got up, lit a pure white candle and played a piece of music — a memory of that past relationship — for the final time, the candle representing light in darkness. A symbolic silent kiss.

'This candle is for you tonight, T.... Wherever you are in the world of Spirit, may you now know the Truth. May you be happy now. I send out love to you now and forevermore.'

I extinguished the candle. Paul left. I am content in the knowledge that I have learned something more about life, to help others. To guide them even more. We all have to *let go* eventually. Forgive — and walk forward.

V

October, 1996

Dear Mother,
I'm glad that I have Paul as my friend. I know that he is going to touch many people's lives with his great mediumistic qualities.

'Oh, hello, Sammy.' (Paul's son in Spirit has just spoken and entered my living room.) 'What is it, darling?'

Sammy's laughing his head off! Something's amusing him, bless him. He's kneeling on the floor right now. He's happy. I've just told him that Daddy's not come round to see me this evening, but he's happy to be here with me while I'm writing to you, Mother.

Rose-marie came around earlier to say, 'Hi' and gave me another beautiful cross. Paul only drew it on paper last night — an exact replica of how the cross is carved.

I gave her a small piece of clear quartz crystal in return. I remember thinking, 'I've got to buy another piece now.'

This evening I went to do a talk on clairvoyance at Rugeley for a local healing group. I was filled with a huge amount of energy from Spirit. I was aware of three people around me throughout the talk. I recall seeing a small child in Spirit drift over to its mother, now guiding and protecting her. The message to all parents who have lost children: God's perfect angels.

'Thank you for those last three words, Sammy. I knew you were here to say something. So I'll write them again:

God's Perfect Angels

I will tell your father that, Sammy. Sammy ....?'

He's gone now. Well, after all — it's long past his bedtime!

After I had finished my talk the lovely lady in question came up to me. We chatted and then she said, 'Who are all those people in Spirit around you? I've seen three lights around you! The energy is enormous.'

On my way out another lady came to me from the group.

'I want you to have this. I've been told to give it to you,' she said.

I opened the little box to find inside a glass crystal pyramid.

'I bought it in Ephesus. I was on an Egyptian Nile cruise and we stopped off there. It's at Ephesus where Anthony built a palace for Cleopatra.'

'Oh, no! I can't take it ....'

'Yes! You must,' and she started to thrust it into my bag. I hugged her.

'Thank you. I will treasure it all my life.'

And I will! So .... I gave away my piece of clear quartz and hours later I am the proud owner of a crystal pyramid.

You *do* get more than you give when you give more than you get!

Drove back home through torrential rain. Got back to find the light on in the small bedroom where I keep my cards and crystals. Strange! Must've left the light on. Switched it off and went into the kitchen to make some tea. Walking back into the hall I can see the light shining under the door. Thought I'd switched it off. Switched it off *again!* Got ready for bed .... back into the hall again ....

'O.k., o.k.! What's going on NOW?'

Yes, the lights are back on again! Maybe I should have stayed in that room. I was obviously being drawn to it. I go into the front room. Wonder what the time it is? I look at the clock on the video — the video that's never been switched off at the wall socket since we moved in, Mother. Nothing! Oh, no — don't say it's gone wrong. I look .... and "someone" has switched it off at the wall! Well, I never!

Don't ever forget! Spirit have a wonderful sense of humour. They love to have fun with us. There's nothing to fear. Just laugh with them!

I now sit in silence holding my cross and my pyramid. Spiritual gifts worth more to me than the crown jewels. I feel a great love emanate from them and know a great inner peace.

VI

October, 1996

Dear Mother,

Turned down the chance to go on TV today. Well, it's such short notice and I have people to see. It was for "The Time, The Place", talking about premonitions. W.A.B.C. Radio want me back twice in November, on the 4th and 21st. Am looking forward to it. Would have been interesting to talk about my experiences on TV, but if you know people who need help that has to come first.

Got my talk for two and a half hours at Cannock library tomorrow, so I've got some rehearsing to do!

The "crew" from Solstice are coming to it too and I do enjoy seeing them all. Looks like being a full house. I shall be wearing your turquoise blue cross, Mother. You know, the one you bought in Capri. Also for luck, spiritual guidance and strength from Diana of Blue Dragon Press. I shall also take my crystal pyramid.

VII

October 30th, 1996

Dear Mother,

Wish me luck, darling, for my talk tonight. Brian, Susan, Gabriela and Paul have shouted 'break a leg!', as well as devastating Diana.

One last look in the mirror .... car keys .... cards .... crystal ball .... o.k. let's go!

I sit in the car outside my bungalow and start the engine .... 'What the ....!'

As I glance back at my front door I see someone in Spirit standing in the hall, waving me off. That's nice. Was it you, Mother? I look again. You — if it was you — you're gone!

Crystal Carole looked fabulous tonight although she had such a sore throat, but to look at her you wouldn't have guessed.

Two years next week since you went away, Mother, so as an introduction for me and in memory of you *Wind beneath my wings,* sung by Joe Longthorne, was played. Crystal Carole is another 'Joe' fan just like you were, Mother. Remember the time I surprised you and took you to one of his live concerts? Oh, you did enjoy it! I recall writing to him, asking him to sing *Somewhere* especially for you that night. So when he began his concert with that very song, it was certainly a magic moment for us both. I also remember the weekend before your funeral and Elaine Longthorne, Joe's sister-in-law, phoning to say how sorry she and Joe were to hear of your passing. We had a long chat. It was good of her to take time out to phone and I know it would have meant everything to you. I know I'll meet Joe one day. I know how much you admired his talents and prayed hard for his health as you and he were both diagnosed at around the same time. Let's hope he will get to read this book one day, Mother, so that he will know you — now in the world of Spirit — will help him with his health and career.

I gave Carole a video of Joe's live concert at the Albert Hall in London in memory of you. I know you approve!

On with my talk! The energy here tonight! The tremendous Spirit activity! Wow! Suddenly it's not "me" standing there. It's someone else. Suddenly it's not "me" doing the talking. It's Spirit!

The first half went really well, although I could tell that my rather naughty sense of humour shocked one or two people. But as I said to them, I am the "Happy Medium"! Life's too short to be sad!

ENJOY YOUR LIFE — AND SMILE!

I have to be *me.* I've created my own style. Shouldn't we all? Nevertheless, I may have been risqué, but I was also serious and tried my hardest to get my personal beliefs out into the open, and what I practice, study and what I'm all about.

After the interval — before I concluded with a question and answer spotlight and some (again risqué) astrological predictions — I got everyone to "feel" the energy within the hall, to give it to each other by holding hands. To believe in Divine Universal Healing Energy. To give away past hurts, feelings and emotions and to replace them with love of self which comes from Spirit and from God. The feeling of energy was enormous, to say the least, and this was something I have been guided to do for people from Spirit for some time now. After it was all over people came up to me and commented on how good they felt, more confident and energetic than ever before in their lives. I knew what I had been led to do was right. It is what Spirit require of me and I am happy to do this for them. You certainly cannot beat a glowing aura!

It's midnight now, Mother. I'm sitting here alone, thinking about it all. Everything is so peaceful. I didn't end up with my head on top of a lamp-post after all. But .... I've got to do it again next week. Then it will be two years since you've gone — and I shall be handing this manuscript over to Diana on that very day! And people say there are no such things as coincidences. I say that this "coincidence" is meant to be from Spirit. To hand over the story of what has happened to me since that very night you passed over — right to the very day. When I had nothing, I repeat, *nothing* to live for.

I promise all of you whom I have met, been able to guide, those of you who love me for myself and anyone who reads this book who calls out to me .... That when I am called to Spirit I shall return, if I am allowed to do so. To help, to heal, to guide. To help you develop yourselves psychically and spiritually. Remember that I shall not forget you. No, not one of you. So don't forget this when I am in Spirit. Speak my name. Call me. Whisper unto me and I shall be there for you. You will know. I shall not forget this promise that I have made unto you. Yet remember that when I am called to Spirit I am called to do other things. To learn even more. To move on. But I shall come to you. Any of you who need me. At any time. You will know when I am with you. For I shall never be far away from you. I shall know when you need my help and my love. My love for you will never pass away — and I shall never forget my promise.

VIII

October 31st, 1996

Dear Mother,

Wow! You should see the colour of the leaves today. Gold, red, yellow, tumbling and falling. Gale force winds shaking the branches with sheer universal energy. I feel filled with energy myself and a powerful feeling of self-control like never before. I know now that no one will ever use me again unless I allow them to. I have so many wonderful spiritual friends now and I'm so thankful to the powers that be for sending them all into my life. So many friends that I can give my love to. I feel very protective of people like Ray and Bridget, Paul and many others for some reason. I know I have to look after their hearts. Ray is one of the most special friends ever to enter my life. He's had a hard life, but now is one of life's givers. When I'm with him talking about spiritual matters I know I'm standing by my brother. A brother whom I once had in a previous life and now in this life we have met again. A great feeling of Spiritual universal life force energy builds up between us.

I've been thinking a lot lately about the significance of my previous life in Egypt as a Spirit Guide — the Spirit of a pharaoh; my being given the crystal pyramid; the visions that I (as well as Ray and Paul) have of glass pyramids, besides being inside them when in meditation; the people I have met that I know I was once with in a past life. (Even my car is an Orion and I was led right to it as though it was meant for me to have.) Today I was shuffling the cards and a card called "The Sage" fell out. It is of an elderly wise gentleman drawing in a book the plans of how a pyramid is constructed and on his desk — a crystal pyramid. This card literally threw itself out of the pack and onto the floor!

Also the Joan Grant books I managed to obtain in August, *Winged Pharaoh* and *Eyes of Horus*. Spiritual significance. All little reminders that I really do have Egyptian connections with my previous existence. All these things are meant for me to know, to possess, to remind me. Why? I do not know. Maybe if I was regressed again it would help me to understand. In time, nevertheless, I shall get my answers. For now I shall just accept and carry on with life. My being an Egyptian guide — and now guiding others in this life. It's as though it's by my feelings that I have to protect and look after my friends; as though I am keeping my arms wrapped around their waists like a belt. Orion's belt.

Maybe in future volumes I will be able to tell you all of the outcome of Ancient Egypt and myself. I may even stand at the foot of the pyramids and then the answers may come.

"Seek and you will find.
Knock and the door will be opened unto you."

The Final Chapter

October, 1996

Dear Mother,
Every day I could write a book about the spiritual experiences I'm having. I found out something else this evening. I don't need a crystal ball or to consult the cards to see people in Spirit. I was sitting with lovely Sandra Field and her daughter in Brian's conservatory. The rain pouring, the wind howling.

Suddenly I see Spirit standing and sitting by just looking at the window of the conservatory, the rain creating rainbows of light from the reflections of the candles. I describe to Sandra what I can see and then glance down at the table.

Two cards have turned themselves over and placed themselves in front of me on the table. Spirit had turned over the cards for me that were meant to be read. At first I look at Sandra, she looked at me.

'I didn't turn them over,' she said.

'And I certainly didn't,' I replied. We both looked at Sandra's daughter. The look on her face tells me it certainly wasn't her. Yet I knew! It was Spirit. Thank you for your help.

I've been thinking as well about the lights going on and off and the video being switched off the other night.

Makes sense really to think that it was probably Sammy. After all, even in Spirit, isn't that the kind of thing a child would do? To have fun with us, to make us laugh.

Also at Brian's, another friend was having a reading. I didn't dare tell her (although maybe I should have) that during the reading as she gazed across at me the table actually rose up three inches and then down again while I was talking about her grandmother in Spirit. Another way of Spirit letting us know that they are present with us. Their choice to be there at the time. I should have told the lady about it, but naturally didn't want to alarm her. I think these experiences are wonderful and I love them, but other people could be afraid, even though there is no need. Always remember than if anything moves in the house it isn't meant to harm or frighten us in any way, unless the Spirit is really trying to attract our attention in a bigger way. Then, of course, we need to ask them what is wrong and how we can help them. It doesn't necessarily mean that if for instance a mirror crashes to the ground it is the work of an evil Spirit. It's more likely to be a Spirit trying to make itself heard. Tell them simply to stay calm, that you will be there for them and can help them.

Ray-of-Sunshine Ray gave me a prediction today for this evening while holding my hematite ring. Something to do with Marilyn Monroe and again something to do with pyramids! Ray claims not to be psychic, but he is. He has the ability to send love out into the universe easily and I know that one day soon he will receive the gift to see Spirit. Everyone loves Ray for the way he is and whatever has happened in a negative sense in his life he has now turned it all into the positive for the love and well-being of others. He is a man to be respected.

II

November 2nd, 1996

Dear Mother,

What an experience! After Ray's prediction I sit in meditation by candlelight with beautiful spiritual music drifting through the atmosphere. I take a couple of deep breaths, prepare to close my eyes to meditate and then .... trance. Eyes open, my attention fixed on my bust of Marilyn Monroe. The large church candle that I have lit flickers as though someone is there, blowing upon that eternal flame. I gaze at Marilyn and suddenly the aura glows and grows around her, just feet away. Like never before.

Then it happens ....

The face of Marilyn changes into that of a man with a moustache and dark beard. "He" is now facing left. We all have guides and guardians. I feel an overwhelming power. I know that I have seen the male guide of Marilyn. Maybe I have seen her as she could have been in a previous life (before her own) or I may even have seen how she might look in the next life. Maybe in a past life Marilyn was a man!

Nevertheless, I saw it. I sat in trance and watched it happen. I actually have seen the male Spirit Guide of Marilyn.

My left hand is outstretched with the crystal pyramid in it. Then I feel a ray — of light, energy, call it what you will — that seems to touch the upper point of the pyramid and what can only be described as an electric shock that shoots up my arm to the shoulder. My attention is taken away from Marilyn to my hand where the crystal pyramid sparkles .... I set the pyramid aside and sat quietly. Then I felt a hand from Spirit reach into mine. Holding my hand. Softly, gently, beautifully. For about an hour I sat with my hand outstretched. Finally and without warning the "hand" goes. My meditation is over.

This must surely have been the greatest, most powerful and moving experience of my entire life. I have been sitting here holding hands with Spirit and watching the guide of Marilyn Monroe come through.

III

November 4th, 1996

Dear Mother,
Due to appear on W.A.B.C radio today. Set my alarm clock for 7 a.m. .... 'perhaps a few more minutes ....' I suddenly open my eyes to find that I am due to leave in ten minutes time! Am now brushing my teeth with cornflakes and combing my hair with the cat! Somehow I make it on time ....

Again, listeners have been phoning me up at home and asking me to tell them everything they need to know free of charge as though it's a continuation of a radio phone-in. Wish people would realize that although spiritually-minded, I do have to make a living! It just won't do!

IV

(Evening) November 4th, 1996

THE GREATEST REVELATION OF ALL TIME

Dear Mother,
I thought Saturday's visions holding my crystal pyramid and watching Marilyn's guide were something, but what I have experienced tonight has been incredible! Candles lit, gentle music playing, Paul and I are in meditation. Again I hold the crystal pyramid in my left hand. I allow my mind to drift back ....

I see the night sky. A heavenly velvet black with diamond stars shining through. Crystal clear. I see Orion's belt. Suddenly I feel the energy from the crystal pyramid shoot through my whole being. I see golden dust drifting down from Orion's belt like a snowstorm. A golden yellow pyramid forms and suddenly I am shooting towards it flying at full speed right to the centre of the pyramid. Collision! The shock makes me open my eyes. I gaze across the room at Paul, who is sitting quietly in meditation. I calm down. I allow my mind to become clear again, breathe deeply and slowly and drift back down into meditation.

I see the pyramids of Egypt and the timeless sands rising as a mist into an ethereal sky. Then I see it and hear it. A powerful gentleman's voice says loudly:

'The *fourth* pyramid.'

('The *fourth* pyramid?' I echo in astonishment.)

As a person would be seen in Spirit, a pyramid more grandiose than the "Great Pyramid" looms behind the other three, surrounded in a rose pink mist.

A pyramid in *Spirit*!

Yet I feel it doesn't belong there with the others. The voice comes through even more loudly and says to me one word:

'Memphis.'

I astrally project from where I am looking at the pyramids to find I am looking at a man with a moustache who I feel I have known all my life.

'The fourth pyramid,' I say to him.

His reply is simple and to the point. 'I knew that. I have always known.'

From looking at him I return to my vision of the fourth pyramid. So this is where the secrets of the world are kept! I feel myself rise slowly and drift on and on. I am being taken by the Spirits of Egypt on a timeless, immortal journey. I stop. I look upwards. I am in awe of the most wonderful sight I have ever seen.

The Temple of Horus. I see the pillars looming upwards into a Nile blue sky. On the pillars are hieroglyphs which I do not understand, being unable to interpret them. I see Horus, the hawk-headed god with wings down by his side. From the pillars an upper beam of stone reveals other gods in a line with each other: Nephtys, Nut, Isis in her matrimonial costume and goddess of the sky. Anubis, carrying a black box within it being the jewellery of Isis. I see Osiris wearing the crowns of Upper and Lower Egypt, carrying the crook and flail. Over to the left of the pillar I see Thoth writing it all down. I know I have stood within the Temple of Horus ....

I open my eyes. Paul is still in meditation. I cannot believe what I have seen. The flame from the candle flickers. I sit quietly, trying to take in what I have been shown.

Have I been chosen to see what no other man has ever seen? What no other man has ever thought of? Why has it happened to me? Why have I been chosen? I recall the dream I had a few months ago that I told Brian about. The one where I saw the plan of an Egyptian Temple in model form. Where Pharoah was showing his son how it was to be built. Where I watched on — in Spirit — thinking,

'It wasn't like that.'

I recall my regression again, when I was the Spirit guide of an Egyptian Princess and all the other visions, the people I meet that I have once known. Only the other day I wrote that maybe in future volumes I will reveal the significance of Ancient Egypt and myself. Even I didn't anticipate this happening so soon.

So now I have another mission. I have to go to Egypt. To Memphis. To Thebes. My quest to find what has been revealed to me and what could be one of the greatest revelations in the world ever to be discovered.

The Fourth Pyramid, where *all* the secrets are kept. Where all the plans of how and why the temples, Sphinx and pyramids were created. When I stand there, I shall know. Yes, I shall know.

I tell Paul of this and I begin to do some research. In the "Book of the Dead" is written: "Then Horus stood over the land. He is the uniter of this land. He is Horus, who arose as king of upper and lower Egypt, who united the two lands in (the region of Memphis), the 'place' where the two lands were united."

I *have* to be regressed again. Yet I know that without asking any questions I am being given clues and answers to what could be the birth of Egypt. I shall go to Egypt now. I shall stand there. I shall know.

I have been given a silver key that I know will open the doors of time. The doors that have remained buried until now. Buried under the sands of time.

V

November 5th, 1996

Dear Mother,
I don't feel your presence, Mother. Not since you last spoke to me. You will when you are ready, I hope. Only a few more days now and then it will be two years since you left. May God look after you and keep you safe in his care. I have my second talk tomorrow evening, Mother. I pray that you will be by my side. I know you will, unless you have other more important work to do.

I now know that after my recent visions of Egypt and from the love that I am given from Spirit, God and all my wonderful friends — spiritual soulmates — that I do not need that one special person in my life. Now is not the right time. Times spent with people such as Ray, Bridget, beautiful spiritual Julie, Paul, Pete, Brian, Sue, Gabriela, Val and everyone else are beautiful times. Evenings of meditation with Paul are some of the most spiritual I have ever experienced. What more can I wish for? I love them all so much. Can't help wondering what else I shall write about to you, Mother, before the next couple of days when this book has to be completed.

VI

November 6th, 1996

Dear Mother,
Again in meditation I have been told two further names: Amenhotep and Cheops. Why, I do not yet know. All will be revealed in time.

I do know one thing for certain: tonight is going to be a wonderful night when I do my two and a half hour talk. Tonight is going to be special. Will anyone be there who will mock me? Put me to the test? God and Spirit will give me the right words to say. Yet everyone has the choice to either believe or disbelieve. We all need to share opinions.

My personal beliefs that I want to share with everyone now, Mother, are as follows:

Out of sadness can be brought forth great joy.
Anger and pain can be transformed into love and forgiveness.
Out of every painful experience comes learning, knowledge and growth to help others.
The Kingdom of Heaven lies within us, also the Kingdom of Hell. Heaven has to win, remembering that love conquers all. It is the strongest power of all time.
Inside each one of us lives God.
And the Devil.

We are tested along this highway of life many times to see how we turn out at the end.
Many times we have to return to our classrooms to learn, to earn our spiritual diplomas.
Inside the darkness of our hearts a candle of light burns — it is never extinguished.
That eternal flame of purity, the God-spark of life that we can mirror outwards.
Letting it reflect out to others to bring love of Self to those who are lost and have stopped loving along life's cruel highway, allowing the world to make them bitter when they have stopped loving themselves.
If each day we can make one person smile, then we have succeeded. We haven't failed.
We have brought light out of the darkness of that person.
For the sake of the Universe.
Universal energy to be brought down from the mystical heavens.
To be shared. Equally.
In love. In health. In happiness.

We are all given the precious gift of life.
Only when we are called to the higher schools of learning can we leave this earth plane, guided by a higher intervention who is known as God to do other work. To be re-born and then learn the reason of life.
We all have the right to make choices.
To believe. To disbelieve. It is your choice.
Yet I do say strongly:
Do not mock others for what they have a right to believe in. Hold your tongue. Listen to what each man has to say. Everyone has their own views and should stick to them.
If you fight for Spiritual proof, you will not get it. All the seeking and searching will not make it happen.
You will find when it is the right time. When it is meant to be. Then, only then, will you get that proof.
When you stop looking for it. It will come. Yes, it will come.

One day, in the world of Spirit, you will know the answers. All will be revealed to you.

This is what I believe.

Do not mock or criticize me or judge me unfairly, like I do not mock, criticize or judge any of you for your beliefs.

Never stop loving. Like Spring follows the dead of Winter, when new growth begins again. It has only been a waiting period.

Love is eternal and the Universe is full of it.

Feel the energy of the Universe fill your hearts, your minds, your bodies.

And your Souls.

Don't forget to listen to others. Be that listening ear.

Never stop believing in yourselves. Or forgiving. Thank God for every day we have been given.

Maybe we can't alter the way the world is today, but we can play our own part in God's almighty plan to give and receive love. To help, to heal and to guide others. To bring forth light. Then journey into the Light. Shine like the brightest star in the heavens.

Then become that star yourself.

Never forget how special you are. And how unique.

Radiate love out and never stop giving.

Enjoy life to the full. Don't give up.

Believe that you are a winner in this game of life where there are many rules.

You will only lose when you haven't tried. Fight on and *win.*

Never forget how much God loves you, and Spirit.

They are not far away from you. Just called away from you for a while so you can make new changes in your life, while they live out a new role. So you can become even stronger through the experiences of loss and sorrow. So you can appreciate pure joy.

At the chosen time you will be together.

Allow them to prepare the way for you in another kingdom.

Be strong. Don't be too proud. It's not wrong to cry. Follow your intuition. Learn to laugh and don't ever forget to pause through life. Stop rushing and stand still. Stoop down and smell the flowers. Look after your heart as if it is a beautiful garden filled with roses.

Take care of yourself and forgive yourself.

Love yourself before you start to love others.

Hold out your arms to those who need comfort. Let your heart give many sad souls solace. Comfort in distress. Love everyone and be thankful to God for your life.

Life, like the Universe, is immortal, infinite, eternal.

VII

(Evening) November 6th, 1996

Dear Mother,

What an evening! Everyone who was "meant" to be at the talk was there. Everyone enjoyed it and the energy that emanated out was electric. You could feel it. Divine Universal energy. Friends like Paul, Brian, Sue, Sandra, beautiful Brenda, Liz and her wonderful family, Rose-marie, Melanie, Doreen — so many people with great spiritual gifts. Wonderful new friend Clive came down from Bridgnorth. He's a man who is going to do great works of wonders for the world of Spirit. A man I know will begin to see Spirit soon. When it is meant to be.

Brian, Sue, Sandra, Paul and I return home for a well-deserved cup of tea. I feel love radiate through the room.

'I feel I've done enough talking for tonight,' I said. 'So many things I still need to talk about. So many things to elaborate on.'

'You can't get over thirty years of knowledge and experience in one evening,' said Brian, always sound in his wisdom. 'Yes, you've done enough talking. Until the next time.'

(The next time?)

Loads of people are interested in the idea of the "Mystic Ed Development School". I know it will most definitely happen and feel that Paul is going to play a part in this with me. Gosh, won't it be exciting to show and teach people the right ways to develop spiritually!

The others leave and Paul and I are alone.

'Nearly two years, Paul. Two years tomorrow — the last time I saw mother alive.'

We talk of friendship and he reminds me of the love that God and Spirit have sent into my life.

Yes, Paul is a true friend. A man who has learned the true value of life through the loss of his son and from the mistakes made in the past. Yet he is now strong. Loving. Through life's hurtful experiences (many of which we bring on ourselves) he has grown wise in knowledge and his belief in God is strong. Like a rock.

I thank God for his friendship. From when we first met he has changed. Love and light floods out from him. He is a true friend and, what is more, he has a beautiful soul.

Paul goes home, I go to bed.

VIII

November 7th, 1996

Dear Mother,

Woke earlier than I expected. A few tears filled my eyes, thinking of two years ago today. The last time I saw you alive. You can't erase things from your memory.

The postman delivers a card. It's from Gabriela, just to say how much she loves me. It means so much. Had a call from Crystal Carole saying that the "powers that be" have suggested that I do these talks on a regular basis. Have to see what develops. I'm game if they are. After all, there are so many people who can be helped and who sit quietly in the audience allowing the messages given throughout my talk to sink in and mean something. Shall definitely form the Mystic Ed Development School now. Can't wait!

Two years. Yes, two whole years. Has it really been that long? *I've learnt many, many things in two years.*

I've experienced loneliness, sadness, betrayal. Users and takers have come and gone. I've experienced hardship. Poor in pocket, yet rich in spirit. I've a share of fame, publicity. I have been able to stop someone from taking their own life. I've been able to heal and to give comfort and love to many and I've been a listening ear. I have turned lemons into lemonade. I have become a channel, an instrument for Spirit so that many people have been able to off-load their burdens onto me. I have faced suicide, disappointment. I have had messages from Hollywood stars like Miss Monroe, Miss Dors and Miss Dietrich. I have been mocked and criticized.

I have seen Egypt and been shown the Fourth Pyramid — a revelation to the world which I know will continue as a quest and that will all be revealed to me. And then, in a later volume, for all mankind to read. I *have* met with triumph and disaster.

I have found my second family that love me for myself as I do love them for themselves. I have turned people away from evil and back to God, guiding them onto their correct spiritual pathway. I have found God again within my heart and have become stronger. In two years I've had many experiences, good and bad, that people don't get in a lifetime.

I've found the true meaning and now appreciate the true value of life. I have become a survivor and have survived. With every painful learning experience I have been able to help others. I have learned how to forgive. And how to love. Through pain.

I am in the hands of destiny and will continue with my spiritually chosen mission. To help people to love themselves and to laugh. To continue to prove to those sad people that their loved ones haven't died, but now live on in Spirit. In another kingdom, that is, God's kingdom.

As long as the breath of God remains within me I shall continue to guide, to teach, to heal. If I can, to be a light that can shine in the darkness of others.

Two years .... Two years ....

Have I dreamed all this, Mother? Will I one day open my eyes to find that you're still here? No. I don't somehow think so.

Love is what we are and without love
We are nothing.
Out of darkness will come Light.

Ten to three. The time you left this life, Mother. Ten to three in the morning. The lasts time I saw you physically alive was ten to three in the afternoon. I kissed you goodbye. I walked away. You passed into Spirit — and I wasn't there.

Yet it was chosen that I wasn't to be there — but the pain will always linger.

(Evening) November 7th, 1996

Dear Mother,

Never in my wildest dreams did I expect this to happen! Tonight of all nights .... The last time I ever saw you alive on this earth plane, I knew something would happen.

Paul called this evening, his aura glowing vibrantly — bright yellow — like I'd never seen it glow before. A brightness that seemed to fill the whole room. We sit, we talk.

'I'm aware of something wonderful tonight, Ed. Spirit activity like I've never felt before in my life.'

I watched lights from Spirit, glowing all around him. All the while he was talking the standard light kept flashing on and off, making Paul pause in between sentences. We smiled and laughed at this, knowing that Spirit was very close to us.

'What can you see?' asked my friend.

'There is the most beautiful white light getting closer and closer to you. It started to appear by the door and has moved slowly and gently over to you.'

'I feel filled with Spirit, can you tell by my voice?' he said, his voice becoming deeper. The voice of his Spirit guide.

Then the most moving experience happened.

'Hold out your hand, Paul.'

He did so.

Little Sammy in Spirit was setting next to his father on the settee.

'Tell my Daddy that I love him,' he said softly.

'You can tell him yourself, darling.'

His gentle voice whispered, 'I love you, Daddy.'

Although he didn't hear, Paul's reply followed. 'I love you, my son. God bless you.'

The tears rolled down my cheeks. I couldn't help it. To see what I could see. To hear what I could hear.

'What's wrong? What is it, my friend?' asked Paul.

I was silent. I could only gaze at Paul with his hand outstretched, little Sammy's hand in his.

'What's wrong? What is it?' Paul pleaded again.

'This is the most moving experience that I have ever had, have ever witnessed. Your little boy sitting by you in Spirit, holding your hand.' More tears filled my eyes as I continued to gaze at them.

'I can feel it,' said Paul, trying not to get upset. 'For the first time since I held my son in my arms when he passed on, I can feel his hand holding mine. All those years gone by and now .... I can feel his hand in mine ....'

I stopped crying. Paul put down his hand. Sammy is now playing peekaboo behind the settee like any child would. Raising his head, then his hand. Then he was gone.

'He's gone now, Paul.'

His reply was simple, moving — a goodnight farewell to his son. 'I love you, my son. God bless you. God, look after my son.'

We sit in an ethereal silence. The emotion of pure joy sweeps over me again. I thank God with all my heart for using me as that channel. To bring Paul and his son together in love, in unity. Together again.

A moment never to be forgotten, one that Paul and I will always remember for the rest of our lives.

Epilogue

November, 1996

Dear Mother,

You'd never know what's gone on since you left .... But you *have* known, haven't you? You've always been there by my side, pushing me on and waving your magic wand, making things happen for me so I can help those in need.

I want my name in lights for *you* so you can be proud of me, but you want my name in lights for *me* now. I know that. So I can continue to work for you by way of helping others to know that there is no death but life. So that I may remove tears of sadness and replace them with tears of joy!

I know that when my work is done you will be there to greet me. To take me in your arms again — oh, what a reunion that will be! Until then I know that you will always be at my right hand side, sharing my joys and my sorrows which we all have to endure. The trials of life that are truly sent to "try us", to see how we turn out at the end. To make us stronger and wiser. More understanding. I am *so* looking forward to seeing you again and my dad, but until then I know that wherever I'm doing my spiritual work, either on stage or off, you'll be there. In the audience, by my side — oh, yes, you'll be there.

I am grateful to you, darling. I'll always be grateful to you for my life and for being the most wonderful mother anyone could ever have wished for.

Our love is immortal, never-ending.
Until we meet again:
I love you. I'll always love you.
Until the day I die — and beyond.
With everlasting love,
your son,
Ted x